talking philosophy

Also by Ramin Jahanbegloo

Talking Environment: Vandana Shiva in Conversation with Ramin Jahanbegloo

Talking Politics: Bhikhu Parekh in Conversation with Ramin Jahanbegloo

Talking Architecture: Raj Rewal in Conversation with Ramin Jahanbegloo

India Analysed: Sudhir Kakar in Conversation with Ramin Jahanbegloo

India Revisited: Conversations on Contemporary India

Talking India: Ashis Nandy in Conversation with Ramin Jahanbegloo

talking philosophy

Richard Sorabji
in conversation with
Ramin Jahanbegloo

OXFORD
UNIVERSITY PRESS

OXFORD
UNIVERSITY PRESS

Oxford University Press is a department of the University of Oxford. It furthers the University's objective of excellence in research, scholarship, and education by publishing worldwide. Oxford is a registered trademark of Oxford University Press in the UK and in certain other countries

Published in India by
Oxford University Press
YMCA Library Building, 1 Jai Singh Road, New Delhi 110 001, India

First Edition published in 2015

ISBN-13: 978-0-19-946288-9
ISBN-10: 0-19-946288-7

Typeset in Perpetua Std 12.5/15
by The Graphics Solution, New Delhi 110 092
Printed in India by Rakmo Press, New Delhi 110 020

CONTENTS

An Examined Self

The Grace of Moral Consciousness

'To be a philosopher is not merely to have subtle thoughts, nor even to found a school,' wrote Henry David Thoreau, 'but so to love wisdom as to live according to its dictates, a life of simplicity, independence, magnanimity and trust.' These words of Thoreau bespeak perfectly the life and works of Sir Richard Sorabji. Apart from being a talented philosopher and a brilliant academic, Sir Richard, for those of us who have had the chance of knowing him personally, is also a gentle and caring human being. The first time I met Sir Richard was a few years ago at a panel on Gandhi organized at the Centre for Ethics at the University of Toronto. He was invited to present his new book, *Gandhi and the Stoics* (2012), which, of course, I had read with great interest. Sir Richard knew of me and of my conversations with Sir Isaiah Berlin and Lord Bhikhu Parekh. As a result, he responded very positively to my suggestion of doing a book of conversations with him for my series at Oxford University Press, India.

It happens that as a conversationalist, Sir Richard Sorabji is a man with a great sense of dialogue who does not conceal his ideas behind great philosophical systems. He is the son of our time, and so his philosophy is our time apprehended in thoughts. Moral philosophy, for Sir Richard, is no exception; it too aims at a comprehension of our time. The best and simplest way to understand Sir Richard Sorabji is to use his own words, from his famous book, *Self: Ancient and Modern Insights about Individuality, Life, and Death*: 'What I see as the ideal attitude is to think that what matters is not the location of our life in the flowing series of past, present, and future, but the quality of our life. However variously different people may assess quality, it is quality, not location, they should be concerned with. And even though something stops many of us from feeling that way, I stick to the thought that that would be the rational way to think.'

As we can see from the previous statement, Sir Richard Sorabji is a contemporary philosopher who argues convincingly against the idea that the individual is a momentary bundle of properties. On the contrary, he discusses self-awareness in human beings as a certain psychological connectedness and continuity. Therefore, according to Sir Richard, in order to not lose our grasp on the world, we will need to abandon the Cartesian idea of a disembodied ego and turn towards an embodied self as the owner of one's own agency and experiences. If this is the case, we can turn to the ancient Greeks (as Sir Richard Sorabji does) and ask the central question on the conditions needed for being aware of one's own state. Through his study of Aristotle, Sir Richard situates self-thinking as the highest order of self-awareness. While studying Aristotle in different books, Sir Richard engaged, during the past 50 years, in wide-ranging discussions on concepts such as time, free will, essence, determinism, culpability, necessity, cause, and memory. However, his work also combines solid and wide-ranging scholarship on post-Aristotelian philosophy of science and metaphysics, and more specifically an acute examination of the works of Greek and Latin philosophical writers, beginning with the Stoics and ending with Augustine and Maximus the Confessor. In one of his books entitled *Emotion and Peace of Mind: From Stoic Agitation to Christian Temptation*, he devotes his attention to Stoic analyses of emotions and various cognitive therapies. All through his work, Sir Richard has tried to read the Stoics from a new angle and to introduce their thoughts to us in a novel way. As he puts it, 'Stoicism can be very helpful in dealing with counterproductive emotion. But it is not a matter of gritting your teeth. It is about seeing things differently, so that you do not need to grit your teeth.' In Sir Richard's view, full-strength Stoicism, despite its weaknesses and insufficiencies, can teach us a great deal about the matters of emotion, conscience, and morality in general. Clearly, this philosophical inclination will work to the extent that 'a valuable contribution of the Stoics was their interest in self-interrogation. This took several forms and one was of only indirect relevance to conscience: "Mistaken judgment might be avoided," they thought, "if we questioned appearances before assenting to them [...]." The Stoics introduced something else relevant to conscience, or rather to the natural law within us, with their idea that we have natural preconceptions (*emphytoi prolepseis*) of good and evil.'

It was in large measure Sir Richard's early immersion in the moral ideas and philosophical disputes of Aristotle and the Stoics that inspired much of his teachings and writings on the diverse but closely interconnected subjects, which became such important themes in his later work and for our time: peace, death, animal rights, and Gandhian non-violence. The Gandhian thought, while perhaps not directly related to any of the themes mentioned here, nevertheless occupies an important place in Sir Richard's latest work owing to his close ontological ties with India. In *Gandhi and the Stoics*, Sir Richard provides his readers with a comparative approach in analysing Gandhi's thought and that of the Stoics on questions of emotional detachment, non-violence, universal love, and personal duties. Sir Richard demonstrates the relevance of Gandhi's philosophical ideas in convergence with the Stoic values. Interestingly, Sir Richard defends the idea that Gandhi was a philosopher, understood in the sense in which the ancient Greek tradition viewed the practice of philosophy as a way of life. In his introduction to *Gandhi and the Stoics*, Sir Richard writes: 'Was Gandhi a philosopher? Yes. He was forever seeking a consistent rationale for all that he did, and, more than any philosophers I have encountered, he subjected his views to relentless criticism, sometimes his own, but more often that of other people, which he published voluminously in his weekly newspaper.' Sir Richard Sorabji is right to think of Gandhi as a moral philosopher, since he invites us more to learn how to govern ourselves rather than coerce the world. Sir Richard Sorabji highlights this and many other similarities between Gandhi and the Stoic philosophers. 'I think,' he says, 'that Gandhi's attitude to politics may have been like that of the Stoic Roman emperor Marcus Aurelius in the second century CE. Marcus said to himself, "If you had a stepmother and a mother, you would serve the first, but you would still continually be returning to your mother. These are what the Palace and Philosophy are for you. So return often and take your rest in her through whom palace affairs appear bearable, and you appear bearable in palace affairs."'

Perhaps the truest test of convictions is that of moral conscience. Gandhi knew that, the Stoics practised it, and Sir Richard Sorabji teaches and analyses it. In his latest book, *Moral Conscience through the Ages*, Sir Richard spans 25 centuries of philosophical writing in order to define the meaning of 'conscience'. Talking about *conscientia*, he says, 'One can say in Latin that a person is sharing knowledge with himself. The *con-* in the noun *conscientia* is simply a translation of the Greek *sun-* (shared with) and the *scientia* is a translation of Greek *eidêsis* (knowledge).' Add to this Socrates's *daimon* (guardian spirit) in Plato's *Apology* and Gandhi's 'still small voice within' as a foundation for his non-violence. Moral conscience has, therefore, a history. But few philosophers have the moral breadth and philosophical depth to write such a history. This is certainly the point which distinguishes Sir Richard Sorabji from his contemporaries. But what is most impressive is that without losing his humility and lucidity, Sir Richard Sorabji is able to rethink one of the central values of our time. As Martin Luther King Jr said, 'There comes a time when one must take a position that is neither safe, nor politic, nor popular, but he must take it because conscience tells him it is right.' If there is one thing that Sir Richard Sorabji has taught us through his work and teachings, it is that there is nothing as significant as human conscience. He has shed new light on traditional arguments surrounding moral dilemmas on the status of animals and human emotions and actions. And he has also tried to overview and explain the principles of *jus in bello* (law in war) through the founders of the just war tradition. Obviously, Sir Richard, as a believer in non-violence and a responsible citizen, is troubled by the present conflicts in our world and seeks to understand and criticize them through his knowledge of philosophy and his interest in the ethics. This shows that Sir Richard Sorabji is not only an Oxbridge academic in the ordinary sense of the term, but also an original thinker of our time, who knows how to harmonize the momentum of the mind with the thoughts of his heart in order to understand the manners and morals of humankind. Very rarely do we have the life of a thinker and reader of the ancient minds so frankly and closely examined as it is in these conversations. One will come away from this book with an 'insider's glimpse' of Sir Richard's life and mind—and that, hopefully, will help when reading his works. As for me, what I learnt from my conversations with Sir Richard is that the profession of a philosopher has the dignity of confronting one's own uncertainties and ignorance. On this, Sir Richard Sorabji seems to have been offering something unique and exceptional. To quote one of my favourite Stoics, Marcus Aurelius, on this: 'The happiness of your life depends upon the quality of your thoughts.'

RAMIN JAHANBEGLOO

APRIL 2015

Part I

A British Indian

Childhood at Oxford

RAMIN JAHANBEGLOO (RJ): I would like to start our conversations with your childhood and British upbringing. So let us start from the very beginning. You were born as Richard Rustom Kharsedji Sorabji in Oxford on 8 November 1934. How was it that you were born in England and not in India?

RICHARD SORABJI (RS): Well, as a matter of fact, we did not come to Oxford until I was nearly four. I was born on the south coast in Brighton. The thing was that my family in the nineteenth century, my father, my seven aunts, and my grandmother and grandfather, had all been treated very well by the British. My grandmother, born a Hindu, had been brought up by Christian missionaries because her mother had died. My Zoroastrian grandfather was very critical of Christian missionaries, but he needed to learn some English to improve his business prospects, and he went to a Christian school in Bombay (now Mumbai) where there was no attempt at aggressive conversion to which Zoroastrians had objected. This was in the 1840s—hard to believe, but it was. The headmaster was such a source of inspiration to him that he converted to Christianity, and the Zoroastrian community was appalled. They resented the fact that this was the third conversion of a Zoroastrian boy to Christianity, and some of the community made several attempts to murder him. At last, he was strapped into a boat without provisions and pushed out to sea. But the boat was washed ashore and found by a fisherman three days later, and he was sent to safety with the Christians in Nasik. Later, he worked for the Bishop of Bombay in Poona (now Pune) and eventually became a Christian priest. My grandmother was herself a Christian, but she founded schools in Poona for all races, three of them separately teaching Hindus, Muslims, and infant Parsees in Marathi, Urdu, and Gujarati, and a fourth school teaching in English. In the English-speaking school, the children were of different faiths, and there was no aggressive conversion of any kind; in fact, there was no conversion. She was apparently a very good speaker and she did raise money for the Church Missionary Society, so they were very fond of her in England. And then my father was sent to study in England. He was there for 10 years. He was sent to school and then he went to Balliol College, Oxford. Of my seven aunts, the first two were refused entry into Bombay University (now Mumbai University) because no women were admitted. But the next attempt was made with a younger aunt, Cornelia Sorabji. She was admitted as the first woman, and she did very well, getting one of the four first-class degrees in her year. As a result, she was expected to have a government scholarship to Oxford, but it was denied to her as a woman, and a question was raised in Parliament: Was this true that an Indian woman had been refused a scholarship because she was a woman? The answer was 'Yes'. Aristocratic women put the money together, brought her over, and she was the first to take the law degree in Oxford. My father came up a year later. They were both protégés of the philosopher Benjamin Jowett, and both studied law. Cornelia only overcame the resistance to accepting a woman student of law thanks to the sponsorship of Jowett. Jowett was committed to teaching Plato's idea of absolute justice to the future administrators and lawyers of India. This is difficult to explain, because the whole colonial idea is an unjust idea; but within the unjust idea, he was committed to teaching Platonic absolute justice. It is quite interesting to see what happened to Cornelia, because within this unjust system, most of the people, though initially very reluctant to have a woman, were very just to her. There were a few bully boys of a familiar kind, but most of them were trying to be just, according to their lights. These are lights we don't agree with, but they were trying to be just, and I think with some effect. So she had a wonderful career. In order to get employed as a woman lawyer, she had to design her own position as legal adviser to the British government on the predicament of women screened from males (and hence from lawyers) behind a curtain, the *purdahnashins*. It took 10 years to persuade the British to give her a job. Lord Curzon had to be overridden as viceroy. The English were kind to her but said, 'Look, a woman can't be a lawyer.' But once she got the job in 1904, she made such a difference to the Indian women she was looking after that most of the British were very supportive after that. So she did have a wonderful life and she did make a very big change for her protégées and their children, but the opposition from some male quarters never stopped. Their background meant that her family was oriented towards England. Cornelia had tried to work for the maharajas, but nobody would give evidence in favour of a woman in the princely states they ruled, even though the maharajas welcomed her. The British weren't happy to welcome a woman, but they had the power to compel evidence to be given, and she could only operate in the British-run states. Given their background, the family was closely connected with England, with others being trained there besides my father and Cornelia. Another aunt trained as a doctor in England, and yet another aunt trained there as a teacher. England had been very good to them in its way. And so, as many as lived long enough returned to England after their careers in India, including my father. Because they were such an odd family, wholly Indian but Christian, neither Hindu nor Muslim, Parsee but not Zoroastrian, it was very difficult to find a marriage partner. My father never expected to, but he married a young English woman, a country girl, after his retirement to England.

Remembering Cornelia Sorabji

RJ: What are your memories of your aunt? Since you mentioned her, I want you to talk about her because she is a famous character in your family since she was involved in the study of law and social work and at the same time in the Gandhian movement and the nationalist movement.

RS: She was against Gandhi, and one of my reasons for writing about Gandhi was because I wanted to make amends for her opposition to Gandhi. But I think from a historical perspective one can understand why she would be against him. In her experience, it was the British who made it possible for her to do her work. The women she was working for were very orthodox Hindus and Muslims. They were behind a curtain, and no male other than their husband could see them; so if they were widows, that meant no lawyer could see them other than Cornelia, the only woman lawyer.

RJ: Why was she anti-nationalist?

RS: Well, this class of women whom she was protecting might own 100 square miles of territory in India. Only the wealthy could afford to live this extraordinary, exclusive life. Poor people couldn't. So what happened when they were widowed was that their male relatives might try to seize the property and murder the heirs, if there were heirs, or murder the widow; there was no protection at all. Because they were a wealthy class, Gandhi's followers—and she interviewed Gandhi on this question—threatened these women at gunpoint to get forcible contributions for Gandhi's cause. And the women stopped being able to help Cornelia, because what she had persuaded them to do was to come out into the open, still screened from males, but to come out and first do hospital nursing and then social work in villages. They were going out in screened cars to teach about childbirth in villages, in places where normally such secluded women would not have gone. She had transformed their way of life as well as protected them. But since Gandhi's followers were raising money for Gandhi at gunpoint, these women were threatened and they didn't dare go out any more, and this brought Cornelia's work to an end. Gandhi was unlike the earlier nationalists. Cornelia knew Gandhi's mentor, Gokhale, for example, very well, and Gokhale was very fond of her. Many in that generation of nationalists believed that the British had a lot of good in them. Even Gandhi thought that actually. He criticized them, but recognized their merits. But many of the previous generation thought that by negotiation they would gain independence. They didn't want civil disobedience because they thought they would get independence by negotiation.

Gandhi and the Parsees

RJ: Many anglicized Parsees were collaborating as civil servants and bureaucrats with the Raj.

RS: As you know, Gandhi's view was that collaboration was the problem. The British ruled only because the Indians collaborated with them. And that was true, but on the other hand, they were very clever, these Indian nationalists of the earlier generation, and they were beginning to get concessions going.

RJ: Gandhi was very close to the Parsee community, just as he was to the Muslim community, but there weren't too many Parsees who collaborated with the Indian Independence Movement.

RS: No, because the Parsees were seen as British or as neutrals. It was difficult for Gandhi to co-opt the Parsees. Of course, they were highly educated and were very useful to the British, and they prospered under the British rule.

A Christian Education

RJ: Did you receive any Zoroastrian education?

RS: I know about it only through friends. One sends me the magazine *Parsiana*. Another is currently the leader of the Zoroastrian community worldwide.

RJ: Were your parents religious?

RS: They were both religious Christians, but who strongly believed in the value of other religions. And that was something I was steeped in—that attitude to other religions.

RJ: Did they take you to church?

RS: Yes. I went to church every Sunday. But I found when I was 16 that I couldn't believe the Christian doctrine, and under the Christian system you have to be confirmed in your faith and acknowledge that you believe these things because belief is a very central part of Christianity. I found I couldn't believe what was being said, so with great reluctance I declined to be confirmed. All my school fellows automatically got confirmed, as it was called, because it was the conventional thing to do.

But to me religion meant a great deal, and for that very reason I couldn't bring myself to be confirmed because I couldn't believe. But I remain sympathetic, and I regret that I couldn't believe. I remain very interested in other religions now that I have a bit more time to study.

Becoming British

RJ: Was it as a result of your philosophical readings that you became a rationalist?

RS: I am not sure that 'rationalism' is the best word for my loss of faith. But my loss of faith was, I think, to do with my being philosophically inclined, although I didn't know the word 'philosophy' at the time. My approach to religion was rather a philosophical approach. I was also very afraid of death; I didn't believe until I was six that we die. One day my older sister said to me, 'You die, you know,' and I said, 'Don't be ridiculous; dying is for butterflies and flies.' I'd seen them on the windowsill dying in the summer, but she said, 'No, you will die.' I said, 'I will prove you wrong. I'll ask our mother.' I went straight out into the garden and asked my mother, and she told me the truth. And from that moment, I wanted to study this philosophically. It led in the very long run, I suppose, after I retired, to writing a book on individuality and the loss of individuality, and whether it mattered or didn't matter if it was true that you lose your individuality and it is gone forever. I suppose I discovered, through writing that book, that there is a certain limit to what philosophy can achieve. I think it did prevent the anxiety about totally perishing from growing larger, because I came to see my fear as something that was programmed into me by natural selection, rather than something that was rational. In fact, I tend to see it as irrational, thanks to some of the ancient philosophical arguments. I came to see it as irrational and that was a help. It didn't mean the fear went away, but it meant that because I saw it as irrational, I didn't have the extra feeling 'How right I am to feel so harrowed'. Instead, I felt there is no rational ground for fear whatsoever, and that kept my fear in bounds. But it also taught me the limits of philosophy, because it stopped the fear from growing, but did not take it away. It might be that art, or imagination, or some religious experience other than philosophy might take it away. But I'm not expecting anything to do so.

RJ: Do you consider yourself a spiritual man?

RS: Perhaps 'spiritual' isn't quite the right word. But I am interested in studying faith and religion and I am perhaps a little too rational for my own interest. But I wouldn't say I'm not spiritual.

RJ: Is it part of your British education to be a little excessively rationalist?

RS: I think it must be temperamental, because it was very early. From the age of six, I was thinking about this question in what I now see was a highly philosophical way. So I think it's probably an individual thing. Of course, it is rewarded in English schooling, but really before I had much schooling, I was already seen by my school as quite rational in the way they approve of. I hesitate to say 'rational', because I am very conscious of some of my many irrationalities.

RJ: Did you ever have a British education from your mother's side? I mean, were you brought up as British?

RS: Yes, I was brought up entirely British by both sides. But in the Second World War, when there was blackout in the streets at night to hide from the bomber planes in the sky, and everything was grey, my wonderful Indian aunts lit up the scene with their brilliant saris. Cornelia insisted they must all wear saris; none of them must wear Western clothes in England, although some did in India—they were proud of both cultures. And they used to come down from London to Oxford, where we then lived, and they used to tell me the most wonderful stories about India and magical palaces. Because I was a little boy, they used to tell me stories about the maharajas, because for a little boy they were very colourful. I was sent to the Dragon School. My view at school was that it is very good to be English, but that was very common; *everybody* was English. Now the thing you lack, you other fellows, is that you're not half-Indian. They got the idea that I had some connection with the princes of India. Of course, I had no connection at all. It would have been good if I had really begun to learn about India. But I wasn't free to go there till middle age.

An Imagined India

RJ: So when you were a kid, you lived in an imagined India.

RS: I imagined an India which no longer exists. It was before Independence, and the princes hadn't yet been demoted. But the real India is so diverse. It is really fascinating.

RJ: Yes, absolutely. What are your memories of your grandfather, Reverend Sorabji?

RS: I never knew him. And indeed my father, who was sent to England for 10 years for his education, didn't get back in time to see him alive. He must have died in 1894, I think—possibly 1895 or 1896. He was born in 1823, though it's hard to believe, and my father in 1872.

RJ: Did your parents talk about the Indian Independence?

RS: No, they didn't. But my father was a slightly older colleague of an Indian nationalist, very important in the early 1930s,

Tej Bahadur Sapru. He is not much talked about now because what he was trying to do was frustrated by Gandhi and perhaps inherently impossible. Sapru asked my father to help him. They were lawyers and colleagues in Allahabad. What Sapru was trying to do might have been very valuable. Part of it was trying to see how the princes could be persuaded to join up with Gandhi's India in a single constitution. They had nothing in common. Why would the princes even want to join up with Gandhi? The princes and the British got on very well; it was a little too cosy, which is why Cornelia got no British help in securing justice for women in the princely states. But it was Sapru with M.R. Jayakar who set up the three Round Table Conferences in London in 1930–2 that tried to frame an Indian constitution bringing together the princes and Gandhi, Muslims as well as Hindus, and B.R. Ambedkar, the leader of the Dalits, who were then called the 'untouchables'. Of these many sides, several said that Gandhi did not represent them. That was at the second conference, the only one he agreed to attend.

RJ: So the name of Gandhi and the news from India were not discussed?

RS: Gandhi wasn't discussed, for or against. It was recognized that he was a powerful force. But my family's hopes had been with something more like those of the three Round Table Conferences, the third of which my father attended and at the second of which Cornelia interviewed Gandhi, partly about the violence among his followers. The great opponent of Gandhi, Ambedkar, attended, and he was the one who eventually composed the constitution as it stands. It didn't accommodate the princes, who lost their wealth, and for a democracy, this had to be done.

RJ: Was 1947 a big date for you?

RS: No, it wasn't a big date, because by then my father and Cornelia were unwell. Cornelia had lost her memory, so they had reduced interest in what was happening. The year 1946 was a big date, because my father's friend and former client, the eighth Nawab of Pataudi, led the Indian cricket team on the first international tour after the interruption of the war years. My father introduced me to him on the cricket field in the Oxford University Parks, and I became mad keen on cricket.

The Dragon School at Oxford

RJ: You started your primary education at the Dragon School at Oxford.

RS: Well, that was almost my first school; I first went to a couple of other schools next door to home.

RJ: What was your memory of the Dragon School?

RS: I loved it. The teachers were so nice and played with you in the playground. They were so funny, and it was a very good, human school. I was very lucky to go there, but my parents were very short of money. My father never expected to marry and have a family, and had not budgeted for that. We did what we could on a little. And after that, I had to get scholarships in order to get good schooling.

Memories of the Second World War

RJ: The Second World War started when you were in primary school. How did you live the Second World War?

RS: Well, those were some of my earliest memories. There was only one cake available in the shops in Oxford, a grey cake, and one stood for hours in queues for shopping and waiting for buses. But no one bombed Oxford, so it was saved from seeing the worst. We were expecting the Nazis to parachute in. It was planned by Hitler, but he had to wait for the weather. So we were given smoke bricks to impede the invaders' vision, and when I was asleep one night, my parents went down to the garden to light the smoke bricks. But actually my parents did not hear on the radio that the date of invasion had been postponed, and so our house was the only one protected from invasion that night.

RJ: Did your teachers talk about Hitler and the war at school?

RS: Yes they did, but not with a sense of panic. We were expecting gas attacks and so my earlier school gave us gas masks. And when the sirens went off because the Nazi planes were coming over, we would get out of bed and hide under the stairs. If the house were hit, we would survive under the stairs, but afterwards we realized they weren't bombing Oxford. So we didn't even get up for the sirens.

RJ: Did you know about the Blitz in London?

RS: The prime minister said, 'Please don't travel; we are expecting something.' So Cornelia couldn't visit us in Oxford on certain days in the beginning of the war.

RJ: Did you see any American soldiers at Oxford?

RS: The Americans came in later, and we quite liked them when we met them, and they were vital.

RJ: You had contact with them?

RS: We put up in our Oxford house the first children evacuated from the bombing in London, and later soldiers, though not the American ones. But eventually the American soldiers were all around.

Studying at Charterhouse

RJ: Later you went to Charterhouse, a famous British public school. Was it very competitive?

RS: It was a very tolerant school. I was a bit of an academic rebel. They were very kind to me even though I was a nonconformist.

RJ: They never punished you?

RS: No. Not seriously. They were very nice to me. I did like them and was fond of them. They had some very interesting people among the teachers. But I think they needed an injection of younger ones, none of whom had been available during the war. In my last year, there came a brilliant young headmaster, Sir Brian Young, who really excited me. It took a lively mind to put unimagined problems to the pupils and that's what I wanted. Recently, I visited Charterhouse, and they are doing well. The pupils were very bright, the school was full of fizz, and fizz was what the new headmaster brought just before I left.

RJ: How were the headmasters? Were they very traditional with a British upbringing?

RS: Well, they certainly had to fit a class system. But the headmaster over most of my time was a kind man, even if not very exciting.

RJ: What was your favourite subject?

RS: I tried to get them to start an English literature department. I got the wealthy father of a school friend to offer a poetry prize, and I collected students' poems for a magazine. But concerning an English department they rejected me, and I'm glad, because everyone could read English, whereas the Greek and Latin on which I concentrated were later to open the doors to Greek, Islamic, and Indian philosophy. So thank heavens I was defeated.

RJ: Did you study Cicero?

RS: Yes, it was a very short period of Latin literature that was considered a good model. Similarly, later at university, we studied at the most 200 years of the 1,200 years of Greek philosophy. In fact, all 1,200 years are fascinating. Later again, in my first job, I was asked to teach in one class the 1,800 years and more from the earliest Greeks to Thomas Aquinas, and I don't think you can understand Thomas Aquinas if you have left out the 1,600 years between Aristotle and him.

RJ: Did you start reading Plato and Aristotle already in high school?

RS: No, and even when I went to Oxford, for the first two years we had to keep reading ancient literature texts in Greek and Latin, but not so much in the Oxford of those days for the literary content. It was more a course in speed-reading. Only in the last two years was I able to study philosophy.

Cricket and the Indian-ness

RJ: What kind of sports did you play while you were at Charterhouse?

RS: As I said, I was mad keen on cricket. I knew the statistics of the bowlers and batsmen and loved to watch the game. When the first summer came, it was revealed that I was no good at playing the game, but I still loved it. My teachers were worried I wouldn't become a scholar because I was spending so much time with cricket, but one of them, Tommy Garnett, was very wise. He said, 'Don't worry; he is putting all the scholarship into cricket, and later he will put all the scholarship into something else.' I always hoped India would win. I still do.

RJ: So you kept some Indian-ness?

RS: Absolutely!

RJ: Was that a problem with your classmates?

RS: Absolutely not. Because I told my classmates all the stories and advantages of being Indian and they believed it.

RJ: Did any of your classmates go to war?

RS: Very much so, with the wars in Korea and Malaysia. I was very lucky. In the year ahead of me in my house, of the six boys, three were injured. One was killed, one was disabled for life with a severed spine, and one was permanently traumatized by being shot at from point-blank range. Two years of military service was compulsory, and in the year ahead of me, it was likely to be at the front.

RJ: And you did two years of national service.

RS: I was a Russian specialist, and it was fascinating talking to Russian refugees all day. We lived in civilian clothes, just talking Russian. We were preparing for later service, but it never took place.

Practising Russian

RJ: Have you kept your Russian?

RS: I haven't kept it up, but I'm sure within two weeks it would come back.

RJ: Are you fond of Russian literature and poetry?

RS: I was always fond, except we always had to read the Soviet literature which was quite boring. The result of learning a language at an intense level is that you become so fond of the people. You feel sympathetic towards them.

RJ: Did you ever go to Soviet Russia?

RS: I did, because I thought I would be a schoolteacher. I went for experience in 1959 and I spoke Russian. But after that I was invited back to the University of Oxford for the postgraduate study of philosophy, then was busy raising a family and making a living, and my first job was in America. I didn't have time for Russian then, and when I was eventually free to travel, I went to India instead of anywhere else.

The Oxford Years

RJ: Who were your professors at Oxford?

RS: I had a very nice Greek and Latin teacher for the first two years, Godfrey Bond. He was so kind to me, and I used to invite him to my mother's house because she lived in Oxford. He used to say that he often walked around Christ Church Meadows in Oxford because the walk was just the right length for dissuading depressed students from committing suicide. I got married to Kate early in 1958, while still an undergraduate student, and under the seventeenth-century statutes of King James I, students who got married weren't allowed to keep their scholarship money or scholar's gown. But he made sure I didn't lose either. After two years, at last I was able to start philosophy. But my tutor had lost interest in the subject, something that would not be tolerated now. I wrote politely to the head of my college saying I had enjoyed my first term of philosophy, but would like time with a different tutor, to hear another philosophical perspective. The head sent my letter to my tutor, who refused to part with me, so I stayed, but privately paid older students to teach me philosophy.

RJ: Did the tradition at Oxford remain empiricist?

RS: Interests have changed and Oxford has some of the ablest philosophers anywhere, but I think the syllabus is more restricted than at Cambridge or London.

RJ: Did you have a chance to go to the classes given by Sir Isaiah Berlin?

RS: I met Berlin while an undergraduate and he said something to me which I thought about for 30 years. He asked what I was reading and I said ancient philosophy. 'Ancient philosophy, ancient philosophy,' he said, 'don't you think the Stoic theory of human fellowship is the very opposite of the Marxist theory of alienation?' Neither of these was on the syllabus. I thought about his question for 30 years and eventually wrote about one half of it—the Stoics. He showed there were horizons beyond the syllabus.

RJ: How many years did you stay at Oxford?

RS: I spent the four undergraduate years, then left and became a schoolteacher. My tutor never said, 'You're good' or 'You're bad'. He never said anything, so I supposed I was mediocre. Fortunately, my Oxford examiners said, 'Why aren't you coming back?', so I came back for two more years of study and then took a job in the philosophy department of a US university. I was lucky enough to get it because not many people knew Greek as well as philosophy in America at that time. Cornell University was my first job, and I could not have had a better way of catching up on the philosophy side.

Living in America

RJ: Did you take your family with you?

RS: Yes, we had our first two children. It was fascinating. It was different teaching, but I liked that aspect.

RJ: How was America in the post-Second World War era? You discovered Cornell in the 1960s at the time of the Civil Rights Movement.

RS: One of my first students, who was slightly older than me, went to support the civil rights voter-registration drive in Mississippi and had people firing at him. England's politics had not been so exciting. What happened in America mattered more. And then came the Cuban Missile Crisis, President Kennedy being shot, and the Vietnam War. The US universities provided the opposition to the Vietnam War.

RJ: But you were not politically active?

RS: Politically conscious only. The entire philosophy department marched down Central Park in New York City with banners against the Vietnam War. Eventually, not at first, almost everyone, not just the left-wing people, turned against it. So, yes, I did become politically conscious.

RJ: Why did you go back to England and leave your teaching job in America?

RS: I had a perfect job. But my reasons for returning were emotional. I felt homesick, not because England was a better place. But my hobby had been exploring old villages in the countryside. I missed the architecture and very historic scenery. I missed that, even though I had good friends in both countries. This was something irrational. I felt homesick. My wife was more adaptable than me, but I was lucky and I got a good job in London.

Back to England

RJ: How different was living in London from that in Oxford?

RS: London had then been cleaned up, the buildings were no longer grey with soot, and all transport was working. It is a great thing about London, unlike Oxford and Cambridge, that you can easily hold intercity seminars, because people can come to London from all over the country and get back home in a day. At a later stage, nearly the entire philosophy department of Liverpool would come down for the day to my seminars, because it was easy. It was easy because trains run into London, not into Oxford or Cambridge. There are huge advantages in London if you take them.

RJ: So what were you teaching? Aristotle? Plato?

RS: The philosophy department I was in at King's College, London, was at first a small one of four people, and so I taught a bit of everything. But when Margaret Thatcher became prime minister, the money for universities was cut and some departments were moved or disbanded. Our department managed to take in an excellent displaced one (the Bedford College department) and became large. I was also able to expand the teaching of ancient philosophy to cover all 1,200 years because now I had more leisure to do it—and even beyond those 1,200 years because I could introduce subjects not taught before. So, eventually, our department could teach every century of European, Islamic, and Indian thought. At first, there had been only four teachers in the department and we could contribute only a little of the ground.

RJ: Who were your famous colleagues at London University?

RS: My boss was Peter Winch, a very able philosopher, an exponent of Wittgenstein, as were my first bosses at Cornell, Wittgenstein's pupil Norman Malcolm, and Max Black. After a few years of enthusiasm, I came to realize that I did not really agree with that line of thought, although I continued to attend the seminars, and Norman Malcolm in retirement came to join us in King's.

RJ: Later, you ended up at Oxford again.

RS: Through the kindness of Jon Stallworthy, my friend from the Dragon School days, and his college, Wolfson College, I was allowed to have various roles at Oxford even before I retired from London. In fact, I was made a fellow of Wolfson, and soon after I retired, they made me a lifelong honorary fellow. Wolfson College was created by Sir Isaiah Berlin for research students and teachers. Fifty per cent of the students were from abroad. Because it is a research college, it covers the subjects that are not on the undergraduate syllabus, and the students are older. Older students may have families, and there is a nursery school and safe play areas. I like everything about this. At meals, there are no separated high tables for teachers and you don't know if you are sitting with a student or professor. They put on the most interesting lectures, seminars, and conferences, and if I want to put one on, they are extremely supportive.

Return to Oxford

RJ: How did it feel to study at Oxford and later to teach there?

RS: I have no duties at all at Oxford, but I have taught Oxford students, and I give quite a few talks there, not as a duty, but for pleasure. It is postgraduate students only whom I have taught. But after retirement from London, I also taught postgraduate students in the USA for the first 12 years, up to eight weeks a year, most of all in New York City, and various postgraduate students or postdoctoral fellows came to Oxford to work with me.

RJ: So what about India? When did you really start having your permanent contact with India?

RS: I didn't have time to go there until 1973. My mother led the expedition to take the whole family to stay with friends. The year 1989 was the other big introduction to India. Before that, I got in touch with the Indian Council of Philosophical Research, which is very impressive. We don't have anything like that in England. They sent me to talk at various places and are still sending me in 2015. In 1989, they sent me for 10 weeks to around 20 universities where I gave 30 talks, and I was a guest, so I was shown how different each place was. It was the most wonderful experience. I admired the universities, I admired what the philosophy departments were doing, and how the Indian Council of Philosophical Research was supporting all of this. In Kottayam, I joined the vice chancellor of Kottayam University, the writer Ananthamurthy, in a run to inaugurate his programme for making the city 100 per cent literate in 100 days, with the help, where wanted, of university teachers.

We were in the Thatcher era in England when nothing was supported and everything was being shrunk. I thought that England could learn something from India which was not then a wealthy country. So when I returned to England, I became the director of a new philosophy centre in King's and designed a programme to welcome the general public to lectures of general interest, implementing the public concern which I had seen in Kottayam. I made a few more visits to India, so far as my busy job would let me, but once I retired in 2000, my wife and I went every year and stayed in the beautiful India International Centre for India's intellectual and cultural leaders. Once again, England has nothing quite like it. At meals, the room is full of poets and film-makers in beautiful surroundings. I found a picture in an art gallery showing the centre's tea room, and there was an Indian lady sticking her finger out from her tea cup, in the manner once thought refined, and she was having tea with Lord Krishna. Of course, the deity was depicted in blue, and I thought: 'Where else would Lord Krishna take afternoon tea but in the India International Centre?'

The Paradoxical India

RJ: How do you feel about India and Indian-ness? What does Indian-ness mean to you, someone with an Indian background but born and brought up in England and considering himself British? Does Indian-ness mean anything in your life?

RS: Absolutely. I think India is remarkable. The friends I made in India mean a very great deal to me. As a country, it is remarkable what happened there. The Independence Movement was absolutely wonderful, and non-violence, properly conducted, an inspiration all over the world. But things went terribly wrong for Gandhi with the partition of the country. It was very tragic and he surely died feeling the whole tragedy. I had to read a book recently about the rapes and abductions during Partition, and it gave me a picture of what India and Pakistan have survived. But India survived and produced a brilliant constitution. I was talking to people in Chicago three years ago and was taken by surprise that some of the most liberal people in the room said how wonderful the idea of freedom of speech was which allowed hate speech. So I wrote a piece saying that people in England and America have something to learn from India because there is a very clever clause in the Indian Penal Code which slightly restricts hate speech but also has a safeguard that deters witch-hunts against religious nonconformity. The clause is that nobody may wound religious feelings with deliberate malice. It is difficult to prove deliberate malice, so it should be difficult to produce witch-hunts. I know that is not all there is to be said, because there can still be witch-hunts if a good law is not implemented right, and I have been indirectly involved in the last two years in a couple of problematic cases. Even so, I think we can learn from each other's provisions.

RJ: Do you consider Indian diversity as a weakness or strength?

RS: Well, it could have become a weakness because it is difficult to handle. But I think to the extent that India handled it, it shows strength. There were bad times under the British when it was very easy to induce religious riots in India. The seventeenth century was a time in England, a small country, when life was very dangerous and hard because of religious diversity and the unwillingness of people to respect different religious sects, and very recently, England has become conscious of such dangers again. India is such a huge and diverse country, and once again, England might learn from seeing how diversity is handled there.

RJ: Do you still have any relatives back in India?

RS: None. They all died. They either came to England or died without children, because very few could marry since they were such oddballs.

RJ: So the Sorabjis (someone like Soli Sorabjee) are not your relatives?

RS: They are not my relatives, although they are great friends. But of course it's a small community and I'm sure we have common ancestors.

RJ: The Parsee community is a tiny community.

RS: Yes, we have common ancestors.

A Typical British Scholarly Life

RJ: You are a member of many clubs, starting from the British Academy going back to the Society for Ancient Greek Philosophy, and many British institutions. Do you feel at ease with this typical British scholarly life?

RS: I do like it very much. You can do whatever you like in the English academic system. The most important thing is that you can invite anybody you like and your own institution will provide a nice venue for them to come, and everyone will think that's a good idea. They may not be interested in your subject themselves but if you are inviting somebody who is of interest, you have support, you don't have to belong to some clique in order to invite the people you like. So I've invited the most wonderful people; for example, I invited an American war hero from America. He suffered 19 occasions of physical torture, most of them deliberately provoked by him, and four years of solitary confinement because he was following the beliefs about inner freedom of the ancient Stoic Epictetus, whom we were studying. I wanted to learn what it really felt like if you were an American prisoner in Vietnam. He was the senior American captive. It was shame that broke people's will. Everybody under torture gives away more than their name and number, and then they are so ashamed that their will is broken and they will comply with whatever the captors want. He said he revealed to his captors more than his name and number, and that they all would. But if you could invite torture again by disobeying small orders, your will would be restored and the captors would lose because they wouldn't be able to make you do anything. This ancient Stoic system worked for everyone who agreed to do it with him.

RJ: Was it at the British Academy?

RS: No, it was at the Institute of Classical Studies. But it doesn't matter where you are. The British Academy would be very cooperative and they have been. I was on the panel for what public events we should have and I think they have become very good at that. Very recently, in Wolfson College, I had a colleague studying constitutions, and his interest was in the seventeenth-century constitution in England. My colleague asked who should we invite to speak, and I said Tony Benn, the honey-tongued doyen of the left wing in Parliament. The college was supportive, although some may have been a little bit apprehensive. But when he came, I've never seen anybody handle an audience like that. The students, of course a lot of them from overseas, were asking questions about Israel and Palestine, always very tricky questions. He was absolutely straight; he said what he thought and in a way that didn't offend anybody, and old people were perched on tables to hear him. You don't have to be in a grand club to ask whomever you like and be supported. That's what I like. So that's a good thing about England. It doesn't even matter if you are in what they call the Golden Triangle: Oxford, Cambridge, and London. Some departments elsewhere are the best departments, and there may be nothing like it in Oxford, Cambridge, or London.

Part II
Gandhi and Ancient Philosophy

Gandhi and Eastern Philosophy

RJ: I thought that for this chapter of the book we could talk about Gandhi and the Stoics. You made an important contribution to comparative political theory by interpreting Gandhi's thought in the context of ancient philosophy and more specifically in comparison with the Stoics. How did you get interested in writing a book about comparative philosophy, and especially in relation to Gandhi and the Stoics?

RS: I have been visiting India and lecturing on ancient philosophy in India for many years now, since the 1980s. When I first came to India, the curriculum in philosophy in most Indian universities included Greek philosophy, but now there has been a move towards more Indian philosophy. Because of this, my Indian friends began to wish that I would say something about India, so I started learning about Indian philosophy. But Gandhi was a much easier subject for me to take because he combined Indian philosophy with Western philosophy, and if he was talking about Indian philosophy, he either translated it himself or approved the translation he commissioned. As a result, I was not trying to understand the original Indian texts. I was not asking myself what the Bhagavadgita really means because for that I would have had to know Sanskrit. But I was asking myself, 'How did Gandhi understand the Bhagavadgita?' My guess was that he had a very idiosyncratic view of it. However, the question I was asking related to 'What did he find in it?'. And, of course, this was a good subject for me to talk about in India because it enabled me to combine Western philosophy with Gandhi's interpretation of Indian philosophy.

RJ: When did you first start reading Gandhi and being interested in Gandhi?

RS: It was because of these visits to India. Vinit Haksar advised me that there was a very good way to find out about Gandhi in the three volumes written by Raghavan Iyer. That was a very good way to start, because he had organized Gandhi's thought under different topics and so you got a quick first impression, and then of course much was available in the 100 volumes of Gandhi's *Collected Works*. Later, I found that there was another 100-volume *Collected Works* online that was a completely different selection and the volume numbers and page numbers didn't match at all. This all helped to make Gandhi accessible, and then I got some more books that went beyond either of *Collected Works*. One of Gandhi's grandsons gave me his new book with extra texts, and a further text I made big use of was *Day by Day with Gandhi*, which was dictation written down by his first secretary, Mahadev Desai, and approved by Gandhi himself. As I worked further and further in, it seemed to me that Gandhi's thought fitted with certain aspects of the ancient Greek philosophy.

RJ: It is interesting that even though you were trained as a philosopher in distinctly Western and British styles, you came back to Gandhi and India.

RS: I realized that Indian philosophy was very interesting. My mother knew Sarvepalli Radhakrishnan when he was in Oxford, and some Parsee friends of his and ours gave me a signed copy of his book, *Indian Philosophy*. I knew a little about India, but I got to know a little more because I was asked to keep an eye on three outstanding students of a successor of Radhakrishnan, when he died. Only two Indian philosophers have held the chair of Eastern Religions at Oxford. One was Radhakrishnan and the other was Bimal Matilal. I had just arranged with Matilal that we would have a seminar together in London where I was going to teach a comparative course on Greek and Indian philosophies. A week before the seminar, I wrote to him asking if he was ready, and I found he had got cancer. So I really got to know him closely only in the last three years of his life, and he asked me to look after his last three students. They were very able people indeed, and they didn't need any looking after from me, but I had the great advantage of getting to know them, and so I have been able to consult them with questions, because they had the languages and were very prolific.

I have to recognize that without the languages my knowledge is quite limited, and I have to be very cautious. In this respect, it is very similar to my imperfect knowledge of Arabic philosophy. But there the situation is very different for the reason that Greek philosophy and Arabic philosophy were part of the same conversation, so it is sometimes easier for me than for an Arabist to choose among the meanings of an ambiguous term, if it is being used to answer a Greek original. That was true of the first translation from Arabic that I read. The translator was criticizing Arabic philosophy as irrational compared with the Greeks, and thought the passage was about ants. It was perfectly obvious to me from his translation that it was about atoms, and was a brilliant reply to a neglected Greek text. It was not true of Indian philosophy that it was typically part of a conversation with the cultures of the West. Hindu philosophy has kept much more to itself.

RJ: When you compare Indian philosophy with Western philosophy, what do you think are the points of weakness and strength in Indian philosophy compared to Western philosophy?

RS: It's hard for me to assess the strengths and weaknesses of Indian philosophy, because of not knowing the Indian languages. My access to Arabic philosophy is easier than my access to Indian philosophy, partly because of there having been one conversation. Greek philosophy was translated into Arabic, often by Christians, for a society made up of Muslims and Christians. It is not such a big leap of the mind to understand what is being said. What I feel when I read translations of Hindu philosophy is more along the line that great minds think alike. In Arabic philosophy, by contrast, the questions are often related, and the answers, though never exactly the same, are answers that fit the very same question. Nonetheless, I do find some accidental similarities when I read translations of Hindu philosophy. When I first read some of the logic, I thought: That is extraordinary; it is so like the Stoic logic, though not like Aristotle's logic. Aristotle's logic focused on complete sentences, the Stoic logic focused on the terms which made up the sentence, and this produced a very different result, closer to the modern Western elementary logic.

The closest Greek philosophy gets to Indian philosophy is through the late Greek philosophy of Neoplatonism, and there is a reason for that. The person we think of as the founder of Neoplatonism lived in the third century CE. He had lived in Alexandria, heard something about Indian philosophy, and very much wanted to go to India, and the best way to go to India was to join the army of Gordian, which set out to conquer India. But the Gordian army got stuck halfway and never reached India. So the founder of Neoplatonism never got there, but he seems to have learnt a certain amount, because he then moved to Rome and set up his school in Rome, and his philosophy has something in common with Indian philosophy.

He had the idea that we have more than one self. The most familiar sort of self, which is rather concerned with the body and has appetites and desires of various kinds, doesn't spend as much time as it might in thinking. But one can learn to identify oneself with a higher self, which is more concerned with thinking, and identify oneself first with the divine Intellect and eventually with the higher indescribable God, both of which are within oneself. These ideas look analogous to Indian themes. Although we know the Indian ones best from a much later date, from the school of Advaita Vedanta in the eighth century, that later philosophy had drawn on much earlier ideas in the Upanishads. For the Greek Plotinus, there are some ways in which you can prepare yourself for the first identification. By studying philosophical argumentation and engaging in it, you may help prepare yourself for identification with the thinker God, but for the identification or union with the highest God, says the Neoplatonist, one simply has to wait as for the sunrise. I took a rather nice photograph on the Narmada River in India, of two priests sitting by the dome of their temple overlooking the river, waiting for the sunrise. The Neoplatonists talk about vehicles of the soul. This is a word used by Plato. For him, the soul needs a vehicle to ride. The stars were originally the vehicles of human rational souls before human bodies were made. But now the soul's vehicles are the flesh and some physical gas that temporarily pervades the flesh, or a physical light temporarily pervades it. The last two can continue to serve as the soul's vehicles after it has left the flesh. These vehicles sound analogous to the sheaths of which we hear a version in the Indian philosophy of some 500 years later. The sheaths surround our atman and conceal the true self. But if one can peel away the sheaths in turn, one would eventually come to the true self, which is hard to describe, but which is identical with Brahman. Again, I feel that great minds think alike, rather than this being part of one conversation.

RJ: Actually Gandhi, who was not a systematic philosopher, was as much influenced by Indian philosophy as by Western philosophers such as Socrates, Plato, Emerson, and others.

RS: I see that particularly in his belief in spiritual liberation, moksha. But everything Gandhi thought or said about philosophy, whether Eastern philosophy or Western philosophy, was given his own twist. He hoped to approach liberation by a very different route. He said that he saw God in the faces of the poor. That is typical of Gandhi: by a twist, he produces a radically different idea. The traditional idea, I think, is that in order to get closer to God, you go into the forest, you get away from people. Gandhi is saying the opposite: You immerse yourself with the poor, you work for the poor, the underprivileged, and in their faces you see God. Gandhi always says something very surprising and he does the same with Western thought. He actually paraphrased in Gujarati, with English translations, some of Plato, and a lot of Christian thought by thinkers like Ruskin, but also Christ's own words, and it always came out different because he had his own revolutionary perspective.

Gandhi the Role Model

RJ: Do you consider Gandhi an ethical role model?

RS: I learnt an enormous amount of ethics from Gandhi and I greatly admire him, but I did learn that role model would be the wrong message to take, because what he teaches you is that if you want to do something on an extraordinary scale in ethics, what you are doing can't be wholly desirable. I will give you the most striking example, as it appears to me. He believed in loving all men, as did Christ, and he carried this out in that he never hated his enemies. I would say he was particularly loving of his enemies; he treated them extraordinarily well. Like Marcus Aurelius, he tried to see why they had views that were sometimes harsh, tried to understand their predicament. I think he succeeded in never hating and trying to sympathize. But the people to whom he was the harshest were his own family, and it would be terrible if everyone took Gandhi as a role model because no human can give the attention that's appropriate to the family if they are also trying to love the whole of mankind. His family was required to fall in with the cause he chose to devote himself to, which was the whole of mankind, but his family took the last place. He actually changed the wording of the Bhagavadgita. It tells you not to privilege your family. You should be indifferent as between your family, friends, and your foes; treat them all equally. That is what 'indifferent' means in that context. Gandhi, in his paraphrase of the Gita, writes in a different word: Your family should come *last*. The Bhagavadgita never said that, but he was expressing a practical necessity. I am sympathetic to Christianity every bit as much as to Gandhi, but the Christians might not thank me for saying that Christ faced the same predicament. When he was told that his mother was waiting at the door to see him, he let her wait and said to his disciples, '*You* are my family.' The truth of the matter is that you are human, and Christians say that Christ is human and divine, but insofar as he was human, it is actually impossible for a human being to attend to the welfare of both family and everybody else. Gandhi was successful, I think, in loving mankind. He was not successful, and he didn't try to be successful, in giving the love that family requires. The world would be a terrible place if people took him as a role model, because families would be neglected, and the world would actually be much unhappier. On the other hand, he is absolutely admirable, and every country needs one or two Gandhis.

RJ: Well, one thing is to read Gandhi, understand Gandhi, and work on Gandhi, and the other thing is to adopt his views in everyday life. Actually, it is very difficult to become a Gandhi.

RS: But I think you can apply him to everyday life because there is a lot of quarrelling at every level. It is very obvious at the international and political level. I am very glad that recently we seem to have become better friends with Iran. But why did we ever make enemies? To go back to a safely distant time, our sabotage of their elected prime minister, Mohammad Mossadeq, in 1953 was completely unnecessary. We have been reaping the disadvantages for some time since. It is exceptional for violent intervention to be productive. We should think about Gandhi in international relations, but also on the personal level. Confronting obstacles in life by anger and aggression seldom solves a problem, and is normally unnecessary. The method of love, in Gandhi's sense, can sometimes work. This is not to deny that Gandhi recognized that violence is required sometimes. What he said was that violence is always wrong, but occasionally, non-violence, for example, abandoning an undertaking to protect, can be even worse.

RJ: Well, as history shows us, Gandhi's ideas were widely ignored following India's independence. His political and economic teachings were especially ignored in India. How deeply do you think Gandhi influenced the consciousness of contemporary India?

RS: Surprisingly little, given what a great man he was and how essential he was to independence for India. His influence has been in the wider world. In India, it was reduced partly because he didn't convince his followers of his belief in a return to village life as central, and partly because he didn't want a personality cult for himself. If he had wanted it, there would have been followers, enormous monasteries, and much else besides, and his influence would have survived more strongly in India, though not the return to village life. But in fact, his influence has instead been absolutely enormous in the world at large. Let me draw from the man who has written more about non-violence on the world stage than anyone else, Gene Sharp. One of his many books is about the twentieth-century liberation movements based on Gandhi. Sharp takes something like 26 attempts at non-violent liberation of a country during the twentieth century, and on his reckoning, about half were successful. Martin Luther King Jr wasn't liberating a country, but he was liberating the black people of America. The most recent example in the twenty-first century, and we hope it has worked, was in Burma (now Myanmar). So that was a remarkable amount of success. There has been an interesting book edited by Adam Roberts and Timothy Garton Ash in Oxford, *Civil Resistance and Power Politics* (2009), which points out that sometimes the success of non-violent movements may depend on violence happening somewhere else as a contributing factor. And this was true of Indian Independence. Gandhi had achieved a great deal by soon after 1930, but after that he didn't achieve much more, and in the 1940s, he left the Congress Party and his influence was, to some extent, diminished. So why was it that by 1947 the British left India? One story is that it was the combination of what Gandhi achieved and the impoverishment of Britain by the violence of the Second World War. That was not the violence in India. It was a worldwide violence on a horrible scale. But when you add the weakening of British power to the psychological effect of Gandhi, it was the combination that worked in the end. But I wouldn't agree with anybody who played down the contribution of Gandhi because he had an essential psychological effect. The British were confident of their own morality, and some of them thought that Indians by contrast were disorganized and undisciplined. I'm not endorsing anything. I'm saying what some British thought, and they were rather good at convincing Indians that the British had got discipline, and had worked out political theory in books that the Indians would need to study before they could govern. Gandhi showed that it was the Indians who had a morality of an astonishing kind. They were, some of them, willing to go voluntarily to prison, or to meet death, without being violent, without feeling anger or hate, which was something quite extraordinary. That was an enormous effect to produce. And, of course, another effect was international. The whole world saw the kind of man Gandhi was. The world thought that India had a morality that was very powerful. All that needed to be added was a major weakening of Britain in the Second World War for it to be no longer capable of running an empire. The two together were needed.

The Gandhian Body Politic

RJ: It seems to me that there is a return to some of the Gandhian principles in today's India through the fasting of Anna Hazare or the anti-corruption politics of the Aam Aadmi Party (AAP). Maybe these actions show us that despite what we said previously, some of the Gandhian principles are still alive in the Indian society, or let us say that from time to time they come back and energize themselves. We had them in the 1950s with Vinoba Bhave, and after that in the 1970s with J.P. Narayan, and today we have it with Anna Hazare and AAP.

RS: I don't know whether in the case of Hazare it's a whole lifestyle that he brings into play. I mean, fasting was just one instrument that Gandhi had, quite a powerful instrument, in some ways—though not the most admirable instrument, because in some cases I have a feeling he used his fasting rather as blackmail. What was more impressive was that his fasting depended on his whole lifestyle, in that he trained himself not to fear death, so it didn't come out of nowhere. It was connected with his whole life. Perhaps, the same was true of Hazare. But certainly, Gandhi thought you had to give up all attachments, for example, sexual relations, otherwise, you were hanging on to something, and then people would have a hold on a part of you, through your wife. But he abandoned every attachment, not only sexual relations, but also the need for food, the desire for freedom—he abandoned them all. Was this true of Hazare?

RJ: No, not really. We cannot say that Hazare is the second Gandhi, but, like Gandhi, he uses fasting as a political strategy.

RS: Gandhi liked to avoid using something that was only a political strategy. I don't know what to make of fasting though, because it seems largely political, doesn't it? He liked what he was doing not to be only political, but ethically desirable for its own sake. I am not sure that would be true for fasting.

RJ: Some interpreters of Gandhi actually consider fasting as a very coercive attitude.

RS: It was sometimes very coercive.

RJ: I think it goes without saying that both fasting and celibacy were Gandhi's forms of experimenting with problematic situations, difficult situations actually.

RS: Yes, but he was absolutely convinced and unwavering on celibacy, wasn't he? And it did give him one obvious moral advantage that he broke the attachment which was the most difficult to break, attachment being what the Bhagavadgita tells you to avoid, and detachment being what gives you freedom from coercion. So it had obvious moral advantages. Fasting itself was slightly more like blackmail, although it wouldn't work if you had not already freed yourself from the desire to live.

RJ: I also think that fasting is part of Gandhi's satyagraha. It's not only an appeal to his inner voice of conscience, but also a strategy to enforce the politics of the body and the politics of the public at the same time.

RS: He did think that truth would emerge through conversation, and people would only come together to talk about the issue under the pressure of his fast. Moreover, it's true that people had to hurry to his bedside to discuss the matter of political arrangements: how they would be represented in parliament, and in future parliaments, and so on. People weren't willing to discuss this except under the pressure that he might die from fasting if they didn't discuss it, and discussion leads to the truth, so there was some connection with truth, certainly. There was also the complication that he felt that it was his conscience and therefore, in his view, God telling him that he should fast, because as he very honestly admitted, he felt convinced that the whole world being against him wouldn't change his mind, that his conscience was right in telling him to fast. But he recognized that he couldn't give any reasons to Rajagopalachari as to why his conscience was right, and he had to admit that it takes a lot of training for your conscience to get it right. How, then, did he know that his conscience was adequately trained? I think the argumentation was actually very weak. He had a feeling and he never really found himself able to offer evidence that he was right.

Gandhi as a Philosopher

RJ: Would you agree to say that if we accept Gandhi as a philosopher, he has two sides to his 'argumentation'? One side is his rational argumentation when he talks about 'the acid test of reason' and the other side is what I would call a physiological argumentation, which is fasting. So we find both these forms of argumentation in the Gandhian philosophy.

RS: I think he was absolutely right to use non-rational approaches, though I think that 'argumentation' would not be the right word. One of the important things he said was that in order to persuade people and get them to talk and think, among the most valuable factors are love, sympathizing with them, not ever hating them, and, if need be, self-sacrifice. If people see you are willingly self-sacrificing without complaint, or anger, these things open the ears to the truth. This is not a matter of having the right arguments. I think this was a mistake Socrates is portrayed by Plato as having made. Maybe Plato was aware of it because he shows how when Socrates refutes people he doesn't ever reform them. People are usually angry when they are refuted, and that is no way to reform people. Gandhi knew that opening ears is not just a matter of having the right arguments. They've got to see that you are not another enemy, that you are not out to make a fool out of them, that sometimes you are willing to suffer for them. That there is a non-rational side to reaching the truth, he was surely absolutely right. I am not sure if fasting was such a desirable way.

RJ: We know that Gandhi was much influenced by Socrates, especially after he read *Apology* of Plato. What was very important for him in the figure of Socrates was the fearlessness towards death. He actually considered Socrates a martyr.

RS: Yes, that's true, he did admire Socrates for those reasons, and Socrates and he had something in common. The day he was executed, Socrates told his wife to go away. He didn't put his family first. Gandhi actually translated into Gujarati, from which it was translated into English, Plato's *Apology*, which narrates Socrates's defence at his trial before he was condemned to death. Socrates is presented as giving a defence of his life, explaining why he has lived the way he has. But Gandhi, in the English translation from Gujarati which he approved, changes things around. He replaces Socrates's statement in Plato's portrayal that the *good* man is always happy, by his own favourite concept of the man of *truth*—it is he who is always happy. It was a slightly Gandhianized Socrates that emerged. But Gandhi was absolutely right in seeing the importance of the non-rational in helping people reach the truth.

RJ: When Socrates says that it is better to be harmed than to do harm, Gandhi considers this as a form of resistance to evil.

RS: But I don't think that Socrates was like Gandhi in that regard. In fact, I found only one ancient Greek who was, because when Socrates said 'It is better to be harmed than to do harm', he was talking about justice, but he wasn't talking about *love*. I found only one Greek philosopher who talked in this context about love. This philosopher was the Stoic in Rome, when Rome was the centre of an empire—Epictetus—and he has one chapter in his *Discourses* in which he includes a discussion of the ideal Cynic philosopher. The Cynic philosophers were not the same as the Stoics, but the first Stoic was taught by a Cynic. The Cynics were very unconventional. The most famous one, Diogenes, lived in Athens in a wine jar because he said: 'You don't need a house. It's perfectly fine inside here.' The clever thing about the Stoics is that they took some of the Cynic ideals about following nature, not convention, but made it a respectable philosophy for everybody so they weren't so eccentric. The later Stoic, Epictetus, in first century CE, is describing the ideal Cynic, and he is saying that if the ideal Cynic is being beaten by others, he will love them as a father loves. That is the only case where I've seen the Greeks talk about it being better to be harmed in the context of love. Love was missing from Socrates. He said you'd be happier harmed than harming others and this is what *justice* is, but love isn't mentioned at all. So I don't think Socrates is like Gandhi in that respect.

Epictetus was an ex-slave. Another Stoic who practised a kind of love was Marcus Aurelius, the emperor of Rome in the second century CE, at the opposite end of society. People were forever plotting against the emperor. But what he said was: 'You've got to understand why they think like that; they can't be blamed.' This was what Gandhi called love. Marcus didn't call it love, though he did speak with appreciation of how the love of his friends was like family love.

Erôs, Philia, and Agapê

RJ: When you talk about the concept of love among the Stoics, are you referring to agapê, which we have later in Christianity and which is re-elaborated by Martin Luther King Jr in the twentieth century? I am not sure that when Gandhi talks about love, he is referring to the Greek erôs, erotic love, but he might be taking into consideration the Greek concept of philia instead of agapê. Which one do you think he is closer to? Is he talking about the disinterested love, or is he talking about friendly love? Is he close to Aristotle's idea of 'civic friendship'?

RS: It's not very like any of the three types of friendship that Aristotle talks about, and certainly not erôs. Erôs is passionate love. Some of the philosophers talked about the importance of passionate love between men, which involves a component of educating the younger man. That wasn't of any interest to Gandhi at all. But it is hard to say that Gandhi's love was like Aristotle's preferred type of love—two friends who because of their good character are very close and well-wishers of each other, each of whom sees the other as another self because of their good character. This is Aristotle's preferred idea of friendship, and then there are friends for business, and again friends for having fun and pleasure. The last two sound much more superficial than what Gandhi is talking about, but even the first is missing something, Aristotle's friendship based on good character. For Gandhi, you have got to avoid hating even General Dyer for machine-gunning trapped and defenceless Punjabis and making the survivors crawl. At any rate, Gandhi sharply reminded his fellow Hindus that, just like Dyer, they made the 'untouchables', now called the Dalits or the 'oppressed', crawl. That attempt to cast even the perpetrator of a massacre in a new light is incredibly unlike what the Greeks are talking about, including Aristotle. Gandhi was not celebrating a friendship confined to good men. Even if people were absolutely wrong in their morals, you would still not hate them, and that's very unusual. You would not find that in the Greeks, except for an odd example in the Stoics.

RJ: There is a great deal of spirituality in Gandhi that you may not find in the Greeks.

RS: Well, you do from the Greek Plotinus in the third century CE onwards find spirituality. I don't know if this had any connexion with his being interested in India and having learnt about India from his teacher in Alexandria in Egypt. But you do find in him a very deep spirituality that is not easy to detect in Aristotle, and is not at all prominent in the Stoics. The Stoics had the view that the entire physical universe was a rational, self-organizing being, which was God, and we were little fragments of that being. But that doesn't often express itself in what we think of as spirituality, except that we have some Stoic hymns to God. If we wanted to find their spiritual side, we would look at the hymns. But only a few hymns have survived, whereas there is a lot of philosophy that doesn't express spirituality. Instead, it is the Greek Neoplatonists a little later who express spirituality and are close to India in that way.

Self-Purification of the Nation and Salvation of the Soul

RJ: Gandhi also spoke about self-purification of both the individual and the nation and he understood this by suffering from untouchability, corruption, communal sectarianism, and so on. There isn't this idea of self-purification of the nation in Christianity, but there is the salvation of the soul. Gandhi does not talk about the salvation of the soul. He refers to self-purification. Do you see this difference?

RS: In the Greeks, you mean?

RJ: In the Greeks, and later on in Christianity and early Christianity. I mean, in both cases, the idea of salvation of the soul is not necessarily the self-purification of the nation.

RS: True, you don't find in the Greeks the idea of self-purification of the nation. You do find in some of them the idea of self-purification of the soul. It is really brought in by Plato, particularly in the dialogue, *Phaedo*, that he writes about the day of Socrates's execution. He makes Socrates say that he is perfectly happy about his death, because tomorrow he will be thinking philosophy and will not be needing to think about his body at all. He had tried to prepare himself for this through philosophy, by neglecting the desires of the body and turning to the pleasures of the mind and thinking. Philosophy is, thus, preparation for death. There is a story about a later Platonist who, on reading this, committed suicide, thinking that this slogan (Philosophy is preparation for death) meant that ideally you should commit suicide. So the late Neoplatonists always have to write a section in their introductions to philosophy that says Plato does not mean suicide. Preparation for death is getting rid of the desires of the body; that is how you prepare for the next life. These Neoplatonists recognized different levels of virtue, and the relevant level was called *purificatory* virtue. Beneath that, the lowest level of virtue was civic virtue, which means the kind of virtue you need for living as a good citizen in a city state, in whatever class you belong to. It is civic virtue that Plato describes in his book *The Republic*. That book is about how to be just within society, but that's not the highest virtue attainable during this life, because the next highest virtue is purificatory virtue, when you have removed the desires of the body, and the model of it is Socrates on the day of his death as described *Phaedo* by Plato.

Purificatory virtue was very well treated by the pupil and editor of Plotinus, Porphyry, later in the third century CE. He wrote a fascinating book with a section describing the Indians. It is a book with four chapters, as we would call them (four books, in the ancient terminology that I shall use) about not killing and eating animals and sacrificing them. Book One describes what the various rivals' views were in antiquity about the rights or wrongs of killing animals. Book Two denies that the gods need sacrifice. It is a mistake to think that the gods are material beings. As immaterial, they do not need even the smell of animals, let alone offerings of flesh. The sacrifice they want is the sacrifice of a pure mind, and this is achieved by the purificatory level of virtue. Book Three is about how some animals are rational, whereas the Stoics had grounded their idea that it is all right to kill animals on the belief that they do not belong to the community of rational beings. Porphyry gives many examples of animals being rational. Book Four is about nations who are vegetarian and have not suffered from being so at all. Their eating habits are described, and this includes the Brahmans of

India. In his reply, Porphyry tried to explain why if you had removed your desires away from your body you would be a just person. On this last point, I don't think he got it right, because he was offering too negative a view of justice. Certainly, if you are not interested in your body but in your mind, it is true that you are not so likely to defraud people or steal their money, you are going to avoid lots of injustices, because it is for our bodily desires that we tend to defraud and steal and so on. But justice isn't merely about avoiding being unjust. It is something more positive than that. It requires thinking about other people: Have you noticed that someone has certain needs you haven't thought about, perhaps bodily needs? This is part of justice, isn't it? You may be unconcerned with bodily needs for yourself. But might not this make you less likely to have thought about the *other* person's bodily needs? You're not being just because you haven't considered that. I think the Neoplatonists got this wrong. We are embodied beings, at least for the moment. They might say we are ignoring what happens next in between incarnations before the next one, or if we eventually escape reincarnation. But it is clear that for the moment we are embodied. If we are going to be just, we have to think about the bodily needs of others and foresee them. Plato's *Phaedo* did not emphasize that because it was discussing not justice but death. Nor, therefore, did it discuss how justice is going to require Gandhi's kind of love to some extent: sympathizing, not hating, nor dismissing.

Gandhi and the Stoics

RJ: Let us go back to the Stoics and Gandhi. From what I know, Gandhi never read the Stoics.

RS: No, he just read a book by a man called Austin Farrar, written 125 years ago. He was the dean of Westminster Abbey, and his book, *Seekers after Truth*, is a description of three major Stoics.

I mentioned Epictetus, I mentioned Marcus Aurelius, and the third one was another great Stoic, Seneca. Farrar is surprisingly good. I might never have read it normally; his is not a scholarly study, but it's a very good account, I think. Gandhi was in prison at the time he read it. He was in Yerwada Jail in Poona and it was already 1924, so his course was set. Hence, he didn't do his usual thing for the Stoics—of changing their ideas around 180 degrees and making them look different. He didn't write about them, although his secretary, Mahadev Desai, knew them. But he did admire them greatly and thought they had got it right.

RJ: Being emotionally detached, as you say, could be one of the common points between Gandhi and the Stoics.

RS: Yes, that may sound very odd because we are just talking about the importance of love, so where does emotional detachment come in? They sound incompatible. But the explanation is partly that the love Gandhi is talking about is not exactly emotional love. His love is sympathy, even for a hostile opponent. Obviously, it isn't passionate; it's not exactly emotional. It requires self-discipline and reflection: Why does this poor man have these views or feelings against what I'm saying? Gandhi tried to talk with a less-sympathetic viceroy about his children and how they were getting on. It didn't necessarily work, but he made the effort and he continued to make the effort. It takes a lot of intellectual effort, which would be like the Stoics, so it wasn't a sort of emotional love, but a very important kind of love all the same. That helps to explain why it doesn't involve a contradiction with being emotionally detached, never angry, never committed to your own life or your family life. I regret to say this, because I do not think you should be detached from your family, but the point is the compatibility of this kind of love with detachment. It requires huge intellectual and imaginative effort and self-discipline, but isn't exactly emotional.

Gandhi and Brahmacharya

RJ: Gandhi is a philosopher and there are comparisons to make with other philosophers, although he is not a systematic figure. But there is certainly one aspect of Gandhi's life that we very rarely find among Western philosophers, and that is *brahmacharya*.

RS: Yes, that's true. But brahmacharya involves a vow of celibacy and that at least is something that had been discussed very much in Christian philosophy. Augustine was a Christian living in the period of Greek and Roman philosophies. He wasn't very good at Greek until later in his life, so he read Latin. But he had access to a lot of Latin translations of Greek philosophy which he read avidly. At that time, quite a lot of Christian couples practised celibacy after they had had their children. Augustine comments on this and says that he thinks it is admirable. But he adds what Gandhi did not observe: that it should be with the full consent of both partners. Gandhi, by contrast, judging from his autobiography, barely informed his wife on the day he took his decision, and on this matter, I would agree with Augustine. I think Gandhi's own celibacy was necessary, but only in the exceptional circumstances of trying to liberate and change the mindset of his country. He could have been defeated if he had retained the normal attachments. But nothing could put him down. When the viceroy sent him to prison, the person who was frightened was the viceroy, not Gandhi, because if Gandhi had died in prison, India would have become ungovernable. It was very hazardous for the viceroy; for Gandhi, it was nothing. He had decided he would not speak on Mondays. If arrested on that day, he would write a few notes with instructions and would go off without speaking. Arrest did not change him in any way. They did not beat him up in prison, or carry off his wife and threaten her. But that would not have deflected him either.

RJ: Would you agree that the practice of brahmacharya for Gandhi is not only sexual but is also taken beyond physical levels, and Gandhi tries to make not only a moral value but also a social value out of it?

RS: It involved far more sacrifice than sexual sacrifice, but was it not the sexual sacrifice that made the rest possible? I read a very interesting case, which made this very clear to me. Some recordings were made of interviews, and recently made available in book form. You probably know the book I mean: *Understanding Gandhi: Gandhians in Conversation with Fred J. Blum* (2011) by Usha Thakkar and Jayshree Mehta. In the 1950s, when Gandhi's memory was fresh, interviews were recorded of some of his closest workers, and one particular couple he forbade to marry. He said, 'I will lose my best helper.' The woman said, 'No, you will gain a helper.' But no, Gandhi would cut her off. Eventually, he allowed them to marry on the condition that they would practise brahmacharya from the outset. Later, he made an even greater demand. I trust that it was not carried out. He demanded that the woman after marriage go to the centre of the most dangerous town in Bengal, at the opening stages of the Partition riots, and remain there for 20 years. I think I recall that's what he said to her. I trust none of this happened. But he expected far more from this co-worker than just sexual sacrifice. He expected sexual sacrifice only of his followers, including the members of his ashram communities, and he was amazed and very distressed that the rule was sometimes broken in his ashrams. But he did not require sexual abstinence outside the circle of his close followers. He didn't, in general, want people even to join the political part of his movement, unless they were confident that they could avoid anger under British arrest or punishment. So he didn't want his rules necessarily to be rules for everybody. One of the great things about him, like the Stoics, was that he didn't think there was one rule for everybody, and that was surely right.

RJ: Interestingly, what distinguishes Gandhi from many philosophers is that his experiments, like fasting, brahmacharya, and satyagraha, get out of the private sphere of the individual and get involved with the public sphere of the masses. This, I believe, is something very unique to Gandhi which we do not find with other philosophers.

RS: Yes, only a few philosophers make experiments in living in order to produce social results, although Gandhi was interested in some Western thinkers like Thoreau and Tolstoy, who did. Many philosophers write about society, but, as Marx complained, their aim may be to understand society, not to change it. Many Greek philosophers did engage in what have been called spiritual exercises, but typically in order to change the individual, not society. In one way, however, this is not so far from Gandhi. He wanted to change individuals in order to change society. That is what was influential, not his social theories about how India should eventually return to village life.

To some extent, something similar could be said about the Greeks. When we ask which Greek philosophers wrote social or political theory, we may think of Plato and Aristotle, along with some lost works by the early Stoics, who wrote about alternatives to the ideal society of Plato's *Republic*. But this type of political theory was not provided by Greek philosophers in general. It offered an understanding of society and recommendations for it, and these might be useful for those who were advising rulers or helping to found new cities, both activities at that time of philosophers. But it was not seen as an agreed method for creating political change. It was by changing the individual, partly by spiritual exercises, that philosophy helped to provide political opposition when the Roman Republic changed into the Roman Empire. Philosophical justifications were already used by some of the assassins of Julius Caesar. But under the early Roman Empire, what a brave Stoic, Helvidius Priscus, had said to the emperor is reconstructed by Epictetus in his *Discourses* (1.2). To summarize, the emperor had told him not to attend the senate on the day he was proposing a new motion. 'So long as you keep me as a senator, I must attend the senate,' he replied. 'In that case,' said the emperor, 'do not give your opinion.' 'Do not ask my opinion, and I will not speak.' 'But I must ask for your opinion,' said the emperor. 'And I must answer what I think right.' 'But if you speak, I shall put you to death.' 'When did I say I was immortal? You will do your part and I will do mine.' Here, the conversation was represented as a historical event. But the Stoics were given as spiritual exercises wholly imaginary conversations to rehearse. That would be true of the imaginary conversation with a tyrant given in Epictetus's *Discourses* (1.1.22–3): 'Tell me your secrets.' 'I am not speaking, because that is in my power.' 'But I will put you in chains.' 'What are you saying, man: me? My leg you will put in chains, but my will not even Zeus can conquer.' Here, as with Gandhi, changing an individual can turn the emperor into the one who sounds helpless: 'But I must ask for your opinion.' It will seem that there was an obvious difference: Under the Roman Empire, there was no chance of an aristocratic Stoic changing the emperor's policy. The emperor had total power. But what was Gandhi's position when he started? He could not know that he could remove the British rule, even though I hope the British were never as tyrannical as Emperor Vespasian.

RJ: This idea of self-mastery that we have in Gandhi, which he calls Swaraj, would have a political inclination, but it is also the self-mastery of the self. Do we find this concept in the same way among the Stoics?

RS: Yes, it was achieved on the whole by different methods, but with the same aims, and I think that the other Greek schools achieved, or tried to achieve, it in different ways. I mentioned two devices the Stoics had. First of all, they had an idea, which I don't actually agree with, that very few things in life matter in the end. What matters is whether your character is good or bad, which they saw as a question of whether you were rational or irrational, since, rather optimistically, they thought that reason played a very big role in morality. The great thing was to *see* what was really good, to see what was really bad, because it was through failing to see and failing to understand that people were bad. In other words, the Stoics were unwilling to recognize that people may see what would have been good but not manage to want it. They further thought that only good *character*, and therefore rationality, were the important things that made you like God. Other things were indifferent. That didn't mean they had no value at all, because there were indifferent things that it was natural and right to prefer if available, the *preferred* indifferents, and correspondingly, it was right to dis-prefer the dis-preferred indifferents. Indifferent things that were natural to prefer included life, health, and so on. Those that were natural and right to dis-prefer were death, sickness, and so on. So it was natural and right to value food up to a point. Moreover, it was your duty to try and secure food, and other preferred indifferents for others, so virtue was intimately concerned with securing preferred indifferents for people. The Stoics were not ascetics, as Gandhi was. They weren't against having a feast, if it was available. But what if food was not available? Well, that may have been dis-preferred, but it was indifferent. That is why you couldn't twist a Stoic's arm by deprivation, if the viewpoint had really been absorbed. The Stoics went slightly further: If you realize that your illness is incurable, you must realize that that was God's will, and then you must actually switch to positively welcoming your illness. You can see how they were trying by this method to get people to have the sort of detachment, invulnerability, and freedom from pressure that Gandhi was looking for by a quite different method.

The Stoic Epictetus explains how he inculcated this invulnerable spirit of detachment in his students by exercises. He thought that what is not in your power to choose is, in his qualified sense, indifferent, and that what is unqualifiedly important is in your power to choose. With that in mind, he told them: 'You must decide what it is in your power to choose and what not.' He sent his students out at dawn, and got them to test their reactions to what they saw. Did they encounter a bereaved parent or a grand consul? They must ask themselves if consulship or freedom from bereavement is in their power. No? Throw them aside then; they are not in your power to choose. This exercise was still practised by the American war hero, Admiral Stockdale, whom I mentioned earlier, and who followed Epictetus in using torture and solitary confinement to make his will inviolable. The idea he exploited was Epictetus's idea that what matters without qualification is under the control of your will; what is not under its control is indifferent. So you must distinguish what is under its control (getting tortured) from what is not (concealing all but your name and number).

RJ: Gandhi does not distinguish between the absence of subordination and being one's own agent, but as you say, the Stoics distinguish between *hupotaxis* and *autopragia*.

RS: The Stoics thought it didn't matter if you were subordinate. If you were a slave (as Epictetus had been, and the Cynic Diogenes temporarily was), it didn't mean you weren't free. Epictetus names Diogenes along with Socrates as two very rare examples of freedom. The master might be the one who was importantly un-free, because he wasn't his own agent; he was constantly looking to see if the emperor wanted this, or someone richer wanted that, and whether he had as many horses as the other fellow. So he had inner tyrants in his desires. He may also have had external tyrants. The emperor could be an external tyrant. But a slave didn't have to have any tyrant at all. He could realize that it was right to prefer life and limbs. But your life or limbs might be taken from you by your master—slaves were often blinded. Epictetus, when a slave, having had his legs broken by his master, said, 'Your limbs are rightly preferred, but if they are broken, it is a matter of indifference.' The Stoics were right to distinguish the question of whether you were a slave and the question of whether you had the type of freedom that they thought the most important. The West has tried to abolish slavery, but has not much addressed the other kind of freedom. To what extent can we compare Gandhi? Was he saying 'It doesn't matter if you are one of the lowest castes, or even beneath that, an untouchable'? No, he thought their suffering mattered and he tried to remind the higher castes that they had duties to the lower castes, and was trying to expand the range of duties that they had. But Ambedkar, as leader of the 'untouchables', was surely right that this was not enough to deal with the injustices.

RJ: We should not forget that it was because of Gandhi that Ambedkar could play a very important role in the drafting of the Indian constitution.

RS: Yes, that's true: because of Gandhi and Nehru. Moreover, the Indian constitution is surely an extraordinarily impressive constitution designed to meet a multicultural challenge beyond anything that we have to accommodate in the West.

Part III

Time, Self, Freedom, and Death

Is There a Self?

RJ: You have written a whole volume comparing ancient and modern insights about individuality, life, and death. Is there such a thing as the self? As you know, the Buddhists have been in debate with the Indian schools for a long period of time concerning the view that there is no such thing as a continuous self.

RS: I think there is such a thing as the self and we really couldn't do what we wanted to do if we tried to abandon it. Even the Buddhists found themselves in a certain difficulty. There is a wonderful Buddhist, Santideva, who in the eighth century wrote that if we are afraid of death we should think, 'There is no self, so there is nothing for me to lose.' All there is, is a train of physical events and a train of psychological events, and these are interconnected, and the train goes on, but the train isn't a self. And it's better to think that way if you're feeling frightened about losing yourself in death. But what about compassion, which is equally central to Buddhism? We must have compassion for suffering. But how can the victim be suffering if there are no selves that are suffering? If something just happens but nobody is enduring the suffering, what does it matter? His response was a very interesting one. It was that when you think you should be more sympathetic about suffering that you must think to yourself there *is* a self. Now that sounds like a contradiction. One moment he's saying to us it's best to think in these circumstances that there is a self and in other situations that there isn't a self. Isn't that a contradiction? No, he says it's not a contradiction because these are not two statements. These are not statements, but medicines. I think that's very clever and very interesting, but I am not convinced by it. For they only act as effective medicines if you take them literally as statements. Compassion for suffering seems to imply someone is suffering. If there were only chains of events including suffering events, why should we feel compassion—for whom? I think that's a real problem, and I think that part of the same problem arises for one of the most interesting contemporary philosophers, whom I admire, Derek Parfit, because in his book, *Reasons and Persons* (1984, 1987), he makes the subject so lucid and does thought experiments which really arrest you. He tries to argue, in parallel with the Buddhists, that there is just a causal chain of psychological events with no self, but he adds, unlike the Buddhists, that there is a brain and that the chain of psychological events is anchored in it, and causally dependent on it. But the thoughts are not thoughts of, or owned by, the anchoring brain, or by anything else. I fear that this would rob us of many things that we want to think. When you intend to do something, you intend that the very same person who now *has* or *owns* the intention will later perform the action. But if the idea of the very same owner at a later date is an illusion, so is the idea of intention. If all our intentions involve an illusion, so do all of our actions, and so too do all our acts of meaning, if to mean something is to intend to bring about certain psychological states in our hearers. Also, I wonder what happens to many, I do not say all, of our ethical concepts. Rights, duties, responsibilities, surely all depend on the idea that the selfsame person made the earlier promise, that is, is the owner of the promise, and is now bound by it. Will not rights, duties, and responsibilities also then become illusions?

RJ: By listening to you, I have the impression that your conception of the self is more influenced by the ancient Greek philosophy than by the representatives of Eastern philosophy.

RS: I think my view does fit some of the Indian systems. It is like Aristotle's view, because Aristotle held that the way to think about the world is to think there are subjects, which have properties. I talked about owning properties, but owning isn't usually the word we use. We ordinarily speak about *having* properties. Subjects have properties, and that applies also to things other than human beings, or animals. A table has the property of being hard and brown, and similarly human beings are subjects that have properties such as doing, feeling, or thinking something. It may be difficult to analyse what this having is, but that is the way we think about things all the time. And the accounts of self that try to do without the idea of something that *has* properties, and to speak only in terms of trains of events, whether anchored or not in a brain, seem to me to get into the problem that we can't make any sense of what it would be to plan what I am going to do. Planning involves considering what actions are going to be *mine*, or what experiences, and how to learn from the past experiences I have *had*. If we leave out this having and had, we can't think about the things we need to think about. And so I like Aristotle's idea that we are subjects who have these experiences, and I think the self is the subject that has them. You don't get a subject without the things that are had, and you don't get the things that are had without a subject having them.

Nonetheless, this leaves room for big differences. Some, like Aristotle and I, think of that which has the experiences and owns the actions as an embodied self. Others think of it as something immaterial, for example, a soul, and that is where many Indian views come in.

RJ: The relationship between what they call the 'atman' and the 'Brahman' are essential to Hinduism.

RS: Yes, but in one way, such things could be seen as examples of what I was talking about, at least in the Indian Nyaya and Vaisheshika systems of thought, which I know you are going to bring up. For these at least, treat atman, the soul, as a unique substance which *has* desires and pains as qualities. They call God *Ishwar* rather than Brahman, but He too *has* consciousness. The big difference from the Aristotelian view is that the thing which has various forms of consciousness is something *immaterial*. The soul would be one example. Nonetheless, these views have it in common with Aristotle that they do not try to bypass the subject which *owns* the consciousness.

The Self and the Stoics

RJ: The entire universe is the self, as it is said in the Upanishads. But do we find the same view among the Stoics?

RS: Not really among the Stoics, but they influenced some later Greek philosophers who did have a view somewhat like that: the Neoplatonists from the third to sixth centuries CE. The man we think of as their founder, Plotinus, in the third century CE, thought that besides our soul, we have within us two divine entities. One is the divine Intellect, that same divine Intellect that created the universe. And then there is an even higher god for these Neoplatonists, the One, which is indescribable. The One is unitary, it has no divisions; you can't break it up into this facet, that facet, this property, that property. It is just unitary, which is why we can't describe it. These deities are within us, and ideally, we ought to identify ourselves not with the soul because the soul is so bound up with the body and its desires. The recommendation is to try and identify yourself with a higher self, first with the divine Intellect within, by intellectual activity, notably philosophical thought. Then, ideally, one would identify oneself with the indescribable One, but you can't do anything to bring yourself to that state. You can only wait for it as for the sunrise, as I mentioned earlier. Plotinus is said to have experienced union with the divine Intellect at least four times, when his pupil, biographer, and editor, Porphyry, was with him, so perhaps he did more than four times altogether. This union can happen during life. It is no good thinking that it automatically happens when you die, because it requires practice. These higher selves are not at all like the selves with which we are familiar, the self so bound up with the body. They are not even really individual in the way our lower selves are. The Intellect is already something outside of time. Plotinus is very honest in addressing the worry that union with such a being would mean a loss of individuality, and I take my hat off to him for trying to answer that very difficult question. But I find it difficult to accept what he says, even though only such an imaginative philosopher could have made the attempt. He gives the analogy of a theorem in a mathematical system. A theorem is something that you prove by using the basic premise of the system, and following the axioms of the system. The whole system would fall apart if you don't have the theorems in the proper places within the system. But each theorem implies the whole system; it follows from some bits of the system but it implies the other bits of the system. The whole system stands or falls together. Now if you concentrate on one theorem in the system, you are adopting one viewpoint on the system as a whole. So, he says, there is a sort of individuality left, because there is an individual viewpoint on the whole. He tells us to use that as an analogy for how you might still retain a certain individuality when you become identical with the divine Intellect. That Intellect consists of intellectual understanding of all the many things that can be objects of intellectual knowledge. Mathematics would be included, but there would be other philosophical truths too. Think of yourself as identifying yourself with the whole system of knowledge. You should think of yourself as identified not only with the knowing, but with the things known. Each mind that has managed to identify itself not with the soul but with the whole Intellect and with all of its objects has, as it were, a perspective on the system from the angle of one theorem rather than another theorem. So it has an individual perspective on the whole that preserves a certain individuality for it in a way. Here, the individual self has identified itself not just with the whole universe, but with the whole universe of Intellect and its objects, and it has retained a certain individuality by seeing it from the perspective of an individual theorem. This goes beyond the Upanishads, and introduces its own concern with preserving individuality. But it provides another form of the idea that the self, or rather the true self, is the universe.

The Stoics and the Indians

RJ: If we take the Indian view according to the Nyaya and Vaisheshika systems of thought, the soul is a unique substance of which all desires and pains are qualities. What do you think is the relationship between the concept of soul, pleasure, and pain among the Stoics? Is their view close to that of the Nyaya school?

RS: We are now moving from questions about the self to questions about the soul. These, of course, are not the same thing, since Aristotle, for example, would not think that the soul was the self. He has a different view from others, both about the soul and the self. But there are controversies about the soul, just as there are about the self, as to whether it is material or immaterial.

To take four of the main Greek schools of philosophy, the Stoics are materialists about the soul. Their soul is a pneumatic gas that interpenetrates your body and exhibits different tensions and wave movements. The tensions keep it together only for a time. The Epicurean school was also materialist about the soul. For them, the soul is a bunch of atoms temporarily bound together within the atoms of your body, but dispersed at death. Plato's soul by contrast is immaterial, although it has spatial dimensions and can move in space. Plato puts a great premium on the immaterial. He thinks that our bodies are an impediment to the best life and our souls would do better to get rid of them. Plato presents his hero, Socrates, as believing that after he accepts execution by drinking hemlock, his soul will be thinking philosophy, unencumbered by bodily needs. He may have thought it could even escape reincarnation. In that regard, he is not so far from various forms of Hinduism. Aristotle, by contrast, says that it is not the soul but the embodied *person* who feels pleasure or pain *through* having a soul. The soul is a *capacity*, the *capacity* for life, in our case for thought, perception, desire, and self-nutrition. That is something we can all agree we have, and his idea is based on biological studies. Aristotle's soul is not a sort of subject, a subject that could go off on its own and philosophize after death, as Plato thought. It could not even survive, when the person whose capacity it was is no more. Because it is a capacity of something, he does not think of it as a self in the sense of the self that I have been advocating. Nonetheless, it is immaterial, because a capacity is not itself a body, even though in this case it is the capacity of an embodied thing.

As to the nature of pleasure and pain, the Stoics were so materialist that they thought of distress as a felt sinking (our 'depression') of the physical soul down towards the stomach, and of pleasure as a felt expansion (our 'elation') in the chest. Aristotle and Plato in their different ways would have thought this absurd.

RJ: At the end of your book on the self, you mention that the idea that the individual self is not independent of other beings can be found among the Stoics and the American Indians. Does this show us that there is no sense of the self without a sense of things being united?

RS: Well, the Neoplatonists speak of the sympathy between all souls, and that's why we have some common ideas. We do have some distinctive ideas as well, of course, but we do have some common ideas, a view that Plotinus may have inherited from the Stoics. Perhaps, he thought that the belief in God was such a common idea. And certain American Indians felt that when they were pounding grain, the grain and they were one, when they were shooting deer, they had to ask the deer's permission to shoot it, and so on. They had a great sense of their unity with nature. When they died, they thought they were going back to the earth from where they had come. I got a stronger sense from this particular example of what it would be to think that all things were one. But belief in an individual self does not normally involve so extensive a sense of unity. Rather, one's idea of self may instead be connected with a particular family, nation, language, or religion, but not with a greater totality.

Death and Reincarnation

RJ: I suppose that this question of death could be formulated in terms of the concept of reincarnation, which you are certainly familiar with because of your Indian background?

RS: Yes, and it is very interesting to compare the Greeks with the Indians on reincarnation. Plato believed in reincarnation. There was another school before him, the followers of Pythagoras, that believed in reincarnation. But there are also problems with reincarnation, which are solved in different ways by Indians and by Greeks.

What problems? For one thing, Plotinus found it hard to square the genetic contribution of parents to the reborn child with the contribution of the child's reincarnated soul. Again, if Pythagoras is reincarnated as Socrates, a later philosopher, that's all very nice for Pythagoras's soul, which has continued. But that doesn't mean that Pythagoras has continued; what has happened to him? The poor fellow is dead; he has bequeathed his soul to someone else. Some Indians and some Greeks argued in favour of reincarnation by saying we can remember things from our past lives. But that is a rather thin connexion. If I were on my deathbed and somebody said, 'You don't have to worry, because later someone else will remember a few aspects of your life', what good is that to me?

But some Indians had a much more interesting idea, to my mind. They had the idea that by going to great efforts in a past life, you could prepare and improve yourself for your present life. And if you take enough effort to improve yourself for your next life again, your next incarnation will be that much better. Suppose you want to be a musician and you made yourself a much better musician during this life. Then you'll start as a little baby in the next life with a better ear and sense of rhythm and you will advance even further. Now suppose we add something to that. Suppose we add a memory not merely of past incidents. You actually remember aspiring to make yourself better through later incarnations and you remember the past improvements. And now looking back, you can see you have got better again. This adds a bit to the story. Aspirations are more central to identity than mere scraps of old memories like some sort of half-dream, half-nightmare. The Greeks never thought of this, and not all Indians consider it. But if the memory is of forward-looking aspirations, now seen to be fulfilled, this makes it more convincing that the improved person really is you.

Plato describes in his *Republic* how you choose your next incarnation. He is very keen that God should not be blamed. It's your responsibility what type of life you choose, and you can do so on the basis of your past life which you remember. He says if you make a bad choice though you had the chance of making a better choice, then it's your fault. God is not to blame. Well, what did Indians think about choice? Different Indian groups had different views. One interesting idea is that although the parents make the body, the soul awaiting reincarnation can by concentration choose the womb.

The Disembodied Self

RJ: The concept of moral responsibility takes us to the concept of 'disembodied self' which we find in Plato. What sense can we make here of the idea of ownership if we talk about a disembodied self?

RS: Well, for a start, I think it would be very difficult for us to enjoy the activities of a disembodied self, given who we are. The things we enjoy depend so much on our embodiment. To enjoy the life of a disembodied self, if that even makes sense, would be very difficult for us. Could we have our present conversation without a physical voice? Could we enjoy sitting in the winter in a warm room and drinking tea? Without conversation, would we not be isolated? Could we converse by willing our thoughts to be received and experiencing alien thoughts entering our minds? Could we know whose thoughts they were, unless they were very distinctive of a remembered person? No wonder Plato advised us to prepare ourselves for life after death, by turning away from the body to solitary philosophical thought. No wonder the Christian Augustine thought the saints would have no memory of friends nor expectation, but be rapt in the unchanging contemplation of God. Can we make ourselves ready to enjoy this? Would I be enjoying this conversation if I couldn't hear or see your smile?

RJ: Do you feel that?

RS: Yes, but so far I have not addressed your question: Could there even be a single enduring owner of conversational activities without a body? Could there be a disembodied subject who *had* conversations? If conversation occurred through willing the transmittal of thoughts and experiencing seemingly alien replies, what should we think about successive memories of having willed the transmission of such and such a thought? What would link those memories together into the stream of consciousness of a *single* owner? Might some receivers of a thought imagine that they had been the transmitters of it and appropriate the transmission as theirs? How would a single owner's memories of transmitting a thought differ from a sequence of disconnected impressions with different momentary owners or no owners at all, each being an impression of having transmitted exactly such a thought?

RJ: So what do you think about the modern denial of the self, which takes the person to be only a stream of consciousness?

RS: Well, I mentioned Derek Parfit, and I have said that I fear his view would rule out forming intentions or taking responsibility, two of the many things, incidentally, which are involved in conversations.

RJ: One of your arguments is that of our agency and our motivation which require continuing ownership of our psychological states. Therefore, what you are saying is that if a person is to play the role of a beneficiary, we first need to have continuing owners of psychological states.

RS: Yes, my arguments about forming intentions, having rights and responsibilities, and engaging in conversations require continuing owners, the same from one time to another. The same is true of benefitting people. Who would be the beneficiaries of a disembodied invitation to resume the conversation (I won't say 'to go and have dinner'), unless there are continuing owners of the invitation and of the later resumption?

The Necessity and the Cause

RJ: Is there a way to willpower, which turns us into agents? Is there a choice without any appeal to such a willpower, or do we always have to appeal to it in order to have choice and to be agents?

RS: I think will*power* is just one aspect of will. And I think philosophers more commonly mention a different aspect of will these days, namely *free* will. But if you look at what they talk about when they take up the subject they call 'free will', they seldom mention the will again, because most modern theories, unlike many ancient ones, do not really retain a role for the will in that context.

Will*power* is indeed one of the ideas that goes into the idea of will and it is still a very much used idea because it takes will power to make oneself stop talking, in my case, or start talking, in some other people's case, if they don't like talking. Such things take willpower and one is much better off if one has got enough willpower. But there are still other aspects of the will. Another aspect that was common among the Greeks and many Christians was that the will was thought of as a desire that conformed with *reason*, as opposed to irrational appetite. But that distinction is not very often made nowadays. These different ideas about will, its *power*, its *freedom*, and its *rationality* were at first found separately, and were amalgamated later—I think, although this is controversial, by the Christian St Augustine after 400 CE.

RJ: I think this brings us to your discussion of determinism, capability, and necessity. In your book *Necessity, Cause and Blame* (1980) you do talk about all these aspects of free will, and you also make the argument that one could separate the notions of necessity and cause, rejecting the idea that everything caused is necessitated. In this book, you show once again the close connection of free will and the concept of moral responsibility. But do you see a difference between freedom on the one hand, and responsibility on the other?

RS: Yes, I do. I think they are very different, because the question of moral responsibility is about liability to praise or blame. A major issue here is whether one can be justly praised or blamed if whatever happens has all along been inevitable, or at least inevitable since before one was conceived. The same question has also been raised about freedom, but here I think it is very much easier to answer. Would one, or one's actions, be free, if whatever happens had been inevitable at least from before one was conceived? There are different conceptions of freedom, and if one distinguishes between them, it becomes obvious that there are different answers for different conceptions. I am not referring here to Sir Isaiah Berlin's very influential lecture (delivered in 1958 and first published in 1969) on two concepts of freedom, which distinguished between negative and positive freedom. He never said that these were the only two types, and in any case, many different types seem to be included under his positive heading. Stoic freedom is only one of his positive types, but Berlin in his lecture denied, wrongly I believe, that Stoic freedom was a genuine type of freedom. The Stoics were discussing what it is to be a free person and were treating it as an exceptional achievement. This freedom was illustrated in Epictetus only by Diogenes the Cynic and Socrates, who had a certain kind of invulnerability. I think this Stoic invulnerability was exemplified by Gandhi and also by Admiral Stockdale, whom I mentioned in our earlier conversation. The freedom consists in being one's own agent (*autopragia*), which is compatible with enslavement in Diogenes's case, with unjust incarceration and execution in Socrates's case, with imprisonment in the case of Gandhi, and with solitary confinement and torture in the case of Stockdale. Epictetus's discourse on freedom (*eleutheria*; *Discourses* [4.1]) explains how through careful adjudication of desires you can be freed from inner and outer tyrannies, so that you are enslaved to nothing—not to house, farm, horses, clothes, furniture, and family. As if writing for academics, he adds books (4.4.1–2), and, finally your own body. That is why you can tell the external tyrant that he cannot put *you* in chains, only your leg (1.1.23). This is how Gandhi remained freer than the viceroys when he was put in prison. Not only does Epictetus regard this freedom as compatible with compulsion; he views it as obviously compatible with the Stoic belief in determinism, that is, with the idea that whatever happens has all along been necessary or inevitable. He thinks that it is so obvious that he does not even mention deterministic necessity throughout his discourse on freedom. The right adjudication of one's desires gives rare people a certain sense of *invulnerability*. This freedom as invulnerability is not the free person's *motive* for adjudicating desires the right way, but the resulting invulnerability is the reason for the person's being described as *free*. Epictetus is right that you can have this invulnerability, even if whatever happens has been inevitable since before you were born.

The main opponent of the Stoics on the Aristotelian side was Alexander of Aphrodisias a century later, after 200 CE, in his *On Fate* and *Mantissa* (23). He makes it explicit in his *On Fate* (19) that he is concerned with a freedom entirely different from the Stoic invulnerability. He wants the kind of freedom that will leave things 'up to us'. In other words, his interest is in moral responsibility, or the liability to praise or blame. A certain kind of freedom, he thinks, is needed in order for us to be responsible for our actions. But this kind of freedom, he says, involves being in control of the choice and doing of opposites in the same circumstances. Or in a paraphrase of the century following Alexander, we would be free only if in the same circumstances it would be up to us now to be impelled, now not to be impelled. To explain his call for this kind of freedom as required for moral responsibility, we need to look at two innovations he made in his *On Fate* (15) and *Mantissa* (23).

Although he mentioned the problem of everything having been inevitable from before you were born, he went further by making a new innovation. He did not think things need be inevitable even at the *last moment* before choice or action. In attacking the last-moment necessity, he went further than Aristotle. His Stoic opponents objected that if things were not inevitable at the last moment, what happened next would not have a cause. I do not know if it has been noticed that Alexander took the first two steps in giving an answer. First, he said that the person's deliberation, deliberate choice, and judgment are the cause. That much is intended to establish his first point, that there is a *cause*. His second point, that there need be no *necessity*, is defended by his observing that we have more than one type of motive. Indeed, we do have different standing motives, and the

Stoics would need to show that necessity has to govern which motive takes effect. To show that nothing need govern which motive takes effect, I need to supplement Alexander's argument with a final step.

The final step is the one that I have earlier applied to Aristotle. For Aristotle, what we call a cause is one of the four types of explanatory factors, and Alexander would agree. I believe the appeal to explanatoriness is a very good first step in defining cause, and avoids the many difficulties that others have pointed out in trying to define cause in terms of necessity. The important point about explanation is that whether one has an explanation and even a complete explanation is relative to the question asked. This is not a point formulated by Aristotle or Alexander. Aristotle indeed thinks that, at least within the sphere of physical science, some things are better fitted for *nature* to explain. But this is compatible with their being so fitted in relation to a *question*, and I at any rate think that an explanation or complete explanation has to answer a question. That question often asks for one fact to be explained *in face of* what appears to be another conflicting fact. To adapt one of my earlier examples, a good student might have two motives: (a) the incentive to attend a good lecture course, and (b) the disincentive if he has to live exceptionally far from the campus. Suppose he attends nine out of 10 lectures. Someone might want to know why he missed one lecture, *in face of the contrasting fact that* he was motivated and the lectures were interesting, or *in face of the contrasting fact that* even unmotivated students were present. There is a perfectly good explanation: the exceptional distance from the campus was always a disincentive, and that was his reason for missing one lecture, to his own regret. Of course, a determinist or proponent of necessity will hold that there must have been some *extra* causal factor on the one occasion when he did not attend the lecture (his children were less well; he was more tired), just as an indeterminist who denies necessity will say that there need not have been. But these are merely expressions of faith, which tell us little more than 'I am a determinist', or 'I am an indeterminist'. The call for a cause of non-attendance is legitimate, but it is met in relation to the question asked by pointing out the exceptional distance from the campus. Moreover, there will be a perfectly good explanation in relation to the innumerable other contrasts that might be raised. There is admittedly one fact that cannot be explained, on this view, namely, the student's missing one lecture in face of a *different* fact: that he attended nine. But why should anyone ask for *this* to be explained, unless it is a disguised way of demanding an apology rather than an explanation? It might be thought that distance does not provide a *complete* explanation, but completeness is also relative to the question asked, and the explanation is complete in relation to the question specified and innumerable others. The Stoic demand for a cause of Alexander's un-necessitated action is met by providing a complete explanation, not by establishing necessitation.

The Stoic invulnerability and Alexander's open options in the same circumstances are only two kinds of freedom. The first is not any kind of prerequisite for everyday moral responsibility, but is a very rare quality. The second is regarded by Alexander as a prerequisite for (though not the same as) moral responsibility. There is no agreement among philosophers on whether it is really a prerequisite. This is one of the subjects on which philosophers have always had different intuitions, and unfortunately, neither side has been able to convince the other.

Aristotle, 500 years before Alexander, did make a further major contribution to the subject of moral responsibility and necessity. He denied the most popular basis for belief in determinism, the claim that whatever happens has a cause. If so, that cause will have an earlier cause in a chain of causes which stretches back to the past or present, and the past or present have a certain type of inevitability, because they are *irrevocable*. If a second assumption is made, that what is caused is necessitated, then the intended conclusion can be drawn that whatever happens in the future has already been made irrevocable by those causes which are present or past, and hence irrevocable. I have controversially taken Aristotle to be rejecting the first step of the argument in his *Metaphysics* (6.3) by denying that coincidences have causes. So causal chains do not stretch indefinitely far back, but are interrupted, whenever a coincidence enters into the chain. He would have had very good grounds for denying that coincidences have causes, given his account of causes as explanatory factors. For coincidences are, by definition, inexplicable. I gave an example: Suppose that five aeroplanes crash on the same day. The government thinks, 'My goodness! Is there some explanation?', and sets up a committee to investigate. Is there an explanation of their crashing on the same day? Suppose it turns out that there were five separate explanations of their crashing on that day: a drunken pilot, metal fatigue, a damaged bolt, a bomb, and fog. What is the committee to say? They found five totally unconnected explanations of each individual crash and of its exact timing. Is that an explanation of what interests the government, which is a different question: Why did as many as five airplanes crash on one day? That would have been explained if there had been a plot to disable five planes. But, in fact, the correct answer to the government's question is that there is *no* explanation of so many planes crashing on the same day. *It was just a coincidence*.

If this is Aristotle's good point—and it is not an agreed interpretation—unfortunately, he spoils it. For he speaks as if, but for the interruption by coincidences, the causal chain would make all future happenings inevitable. This is to concede unnecessarily that whatever is caused is necessitated. Good as is his denial that whatever happens has a cause, he also needs the other point that was extrapolated from his views: Since a cause is an explanatory factor, there is no requirement that what is caused is always necessitated, because even complete explanations do not have to necessitate. They may or may not do so.

What Is Time?

RJ: I think that we should bring in the notion of time. We have different concepts of time. We have a linear concept of time, but we also have a cyclical concept of time. These are different forms of approaching time. In Indian ethics, we have a circular time, not a linear time. So there is no sense of progress, going from the past to the future. We have the creation and destruction of the world. Take, for example, the notion of the Kali Yuga, which is the last of the four stages the world goes through as part of the cycle of yugas. This is the whole difference between Eastern philosophy and Western philosophy. The Western civilization is based on the notion of linear time and progress without which we would not have modern science and modern technology.

RS: Usually, when people talk of time being circular, they only mean that *events* go round in a circle, not time *itself*, although we can find possible exceptions in Greek thought. I am not aware of exceptions in Indian thought. There is an Indian idea of repeated dissolution and recreation of the world. It is found in the Puranas and in much Hindu philosophy. But, as Anindita Balslev has pointed out in *A Study of Time in Indian Philosophy* (1983), it is far from any Greek idea of exact repetition and it allows for moral progress and final salvation. The Bhagavadgita (8.16) says: 'From the world of Brahma down, all the worlds are subject to return, O Arjuna, but on coming to Me there is *no rebirth*.'

Among the Greeks, by contrast, the Stoics thought that the universe would repeat its history exactly, and we would sit here and have the same conversation an infinity of times in the future, and we've already done so an infinity of times in the past, but never remembering the previous ones. But even they did not end up with circular time, I believe. They thought of time as a straight line with the *events* recurring exactly the same way cyclically. You are right that determinism, the belief that whatever happens has all along been inevitable, is relevant to such beliefs. The Stoics could only make the idea of endless repetition plausible through their deterministic belief in inevitability. Otherwise, it would be too much of a giant coincidence that events would repeat themselves exactly even once, let alone an infinity of times.

Something like the idea of time itself being circular is described in the pseudo-Aristotelian *Problems*, from Aristotle's school, but only in order to present it as absurd. This work describes and rejects an argument according to which we are earlier (as well as later) than an ancient war, the war of the Greeks against Troy, because things are circular. Unfortunately, the argument unjustifiably supports the idea of our being earlier by postulating a beginning and suggesting that we might be nearer to it than the people of Troy. The pseudo-Aristotelian author then has no difficulty in dismissing the argument, thus distorted, by pointing out that a circle has no beginning. What is very interesting, however, is that he compares a remark of Alcmaeon, an earlier associate of the Pythagoreans of the fifth century BCE. Alcmaeon suggests that people die because they are not able to join their beginning to their end. The way I interpret this much debated saying is that Alcmaeon means humans would be immortal if they could dwindle down into the very same seeds from which they came. Might not this be possible if we took seriously the idea of circular time in *Problems*, and thought that the circle was short, lasting, say, only 40 years? Each person in circular time would then live in the world both before and after their one and only birth. If the circle were a big one, they would spend a long time dead before the arrival of their one and only birth. The value of a short 40-year cycle and of dwindling down into the very same seeds from which they came would be that there would be no time during which they were non-existent. They would, in Alcmaeon's words, have joined their beginning to their end and would be immortal. It is not that Alcmaeon had thought this out. He too speaks of such immortality as something impossible. But when he is quoted in conjunction with the idea of circular time, we begin to see how time, if circular, could make Alcmaeon's imaginary immortality possible.

This idea also has implications for determinism. In circular time, everything, and not only my birth, would lie in both past and future. Should we think that since it lies in the past, it is irrevocable? Or should we think that since it lies in the future it is not irrevocable? I'm inclined to think that we should draw the second conclusion. I am not sure that anything that was genuinely circular would be irrevocable in time, because to say that things are irrevocable is to say that no matter what I do in the future I can't bring it about that the past is different. Now, would that be true in circular time? In circular time, it may be impossible for me to do something different in the future, but if I *were* to do something different in the future, then the past would *have* been different. So I am not sure that by this definition of irrevocability anything would be irrevocable in circular time.

Time and Consolation

RJ: Do the Stoics have a sense of history and progress?

RS: No, it has been said that Christianity introduced a much stronger idea of the *world's* progress than the Greeks had before. Of course, progress was very important to some of the Greek and Roman philosophers, but what they encouraged was progress *within* a single life, and that idea was borrowed by Christianity. John Bunyan's seventeenth-century *Pilgrim's Progress* is one of the most famous books of English Christian literature. It's about the life of a pilgrim, written by a man with a burdensome sense of sin, who wanted, however, to progress through all temptations and reach heaven despite his sinfulness. He took the idea of a life of progress from the ancient Greeks. He took it from a Pythagorean text, *The Table of Cebes*. But the idea that the whole *universe* is progressing is impossible for the Stoics because events would repeat themselves exactly. So they couldn't have the Christian hope of world progress, and they didn't use the idea of eternal return to cheer people up and tell them that they would never be finally dead. Instead, the Roman Stoics thought that the occurrence of certain recent catastrophes was a sign of the approach of the periodic great catastrophe: the destruction of the cosmic order, as we know it, in a giant conflagration. The Christians, by contrast, believed in progress. Christ would come again, and some would go to heaven, others to hell, and justice would be done.

RJ: Which concept of time do you feel very close to? Is it the existential concept of time, meaning time as duration? Or is it time as onward progress—I mean, the progress of civilization, science, and technologies?

RS: The history of evolution on earth and in the wider cosmos does not make one confident of progress. The commercial exploitation of technology actually threatens the continuation of the human race, and bacteria may be fitter than humans for surviving climate change. I am interested in time in the universe. I feel small at the thought of infinite time, at the thought that the universe we know may, like me, be mortal, that it may not be the only universe. We are far from being the centre of the universe, as was once thought.

RJ: When we talk about time, one of the aspects that comes up and you mention in your writings is peace of mind and the anticipation of misfortune. This is a way of approaching time as consolation. It is time we need to *accommodate ourselves to* pain. The Epicureans were against this, but it was a very crucial concept for the Stoics, because anticipation has the same effect as lapse of time on those who have not anticipated; it gives time for reflection and for correcting one's evaluation of the situation.

RS: The Epicureans had a different view from the Stoics, that it gave joy to anticipate true pleasures and to recollect them. Epicurus wrote on the last day of his life that recalling the pleasure of the past philosophical conversations gave him joy, which counterbalanced the intense pain of terminal strangury, a blocked bladder. He thought true pleasure was the absence of pain and the counterbalancing was presumably enough to cancel the physical pain. In other words, Epicurus too used thought about the past or future to provide consolation. But the pleasure he sought, the absence of pain, was, in his view, attainable. The Stoics had the same interest in avoiding distress, but did not agree that that would amount to pleasure, which they considered an irrational emotion. The Stoic Epictetus recommended avoiding the eventual distress of bereavement by saying to yourself as you kiss your wife that you are kissing a mortal. But the Stoics agreed with the Epicureans that you should not *fear* future death. One value of *anticipating* it is that the unexpected causes shock, which misleads you into thinking that what has happened is evil, when it is not. There was a case of a man in England who thought he had won the national lottery, but he had misremembered the numbers. When he found he hadn't won, he committed suicide. Why? He hadn't won the previous week, or the week before that. What was different? Nothing was different except his false expectation. He committed suicide because he thought the unexpected was bad, but it wasn't really any worse than the previous week. Cicero, who reports the Stoics, gives a further reason why anticipation can help. Anticipation, he says, has the same effect as lapse of time, which dims any sense of harm. By anticipating, you can gain this sense of harmlessness in advance.

RJ: Our relation to the future is a relation to the expected and the unexpected, because death is expected, death is an expectation. It is a horizon of expectation for human beings. So it brings us to this key question: Why should humans worry so much about what is going to happen in the future but not worry about the past? What is it that we worry about since it will happen in the future and when we are non-existent?

RS: Indeed, some people, and I said in our first talk that I am one of them, do feel a sort of horror at the idea of being extinguished in the future, losing their identity, and yet why don't we feel horror, most of us, at the fact that we didn't exist before we were conceived. Isn't that irrational? Are past and future non-existence not mirror images of each other? I came to the conclusion in *Time, Creation and the Continuum* (1983) that, insofar as the fear is only the fear of future non-existence (there are other reasons why death is feared), it is irrational to treat that differently from past non-existence. But natural selection has caused us to treat future non-existence as more important. Children who exhibited the opposite valuation would not have lived long enough to pass on their genes. So those whom natural selection has endowed with a somewhat excessive aversion to future non-existence will not find that it simply goes away, when they realize that it is caused, rather than being based on rational reasons. For natural selection is a very powerful cause. Nonetheless, the recognition that excessive aversion is not rationally based at least stops any horror from increasing. For one does not say to oneself, 'How right I am to be horrified'. Instead, one recognizes that the attitude has natural causes. That emotions tend to increase if they are considered justified was noticed by the nineteenth-century psychologist, William James. 'We don't cry,' he said, 'because we are sad; we are sad because we cry.' Our mistake, he was saying, is to regard a natural reaction to unpleasant news as a justification for actual sadness. To the thought of our future non-existence, horror is a natural, though not a universal, reaction. The recognition that the horror does not have a rational justification prevents the horror from growing, but does not remove it. There is a limit to what philosophy can do. I think it would have to be something other than philosophy that takes the horror away if you were one of those people who experiences it. But philosophical thought can prevent it from growing.

Death and Will to Life: East and West

RJ: Isn't it because we have this Schopenhauerian will to life which somehow possesses us with its power by pushing us to grab the essence of life and not wanting to die?

RS: It's difficult to know why it happens, but I think it is partly cultural because of the variations I have noticed. My initial experience, when I talked about horror at future non-existence with people, and often with non-academic people rather than with students, was that most groups divided half and half, as to whether they felt any horror. I was usually in England or America, and half didn't feel any horror at all. But then I noticed that there were differences. I noticed it first rather strongly, when I spoke regularly with a group of nurses who invited me to talk philosophy with them. And I talked about what I happened to be researching at the moment. Then I thought, 'How selfish of me to talk about what happens to interest me at the moment', and I chose a subject instead that I thought would interest them as nurses: Is it irrational to fear future non-existence? It was the first time that none of them was interested. They said, 'What's the problem?' I think this was because they were dealing with death every day and couldn't afford to think about it. They gave the best care they possibly could; that was all they had time to consider.

RJ: In a technical way?

RS: Yes, because they had to do that. If they were upset about non-existence, they couldn't do their jobs properly. The other place where I found no reaction was among students in India, where Hindus believe in reincarnation, and had no reason to contemplate non-existence. Moreover, in Hinduism, reincarnation is thought of as a natural outcome, unlike Christian resurrection of the body, which requires belief in the miraculous intervention of a superhuman deity. So I think there may be something cultural about it. In the USA, I think the culture has changed. I was giving a seminar in New York a few years ago and I raised the question whether it was irrational to fear future non-existence. The entire audience, of very mixed religions—Jewish, very different branches of Christianity, a Buddhist among them—did not find the question interesting. And one very, very kind woman in the room said in a sympathetic voice, 'You must be worried because you are so near death.' I still meet people who feel horror, and then I'm very happy to talk to them. But now I wait for them to ask me.

Thinking the Universe

RJ: Well, to escape the horror of death, human beings created religions and this brings us back to the concept of time. Religion tries to explain our past, and also our future after death. Once again, we go back to the question of salvation and ask questions such as: Does the universe have an infinite past or not? What is time in the universe? These questions have also been part of your scholarly research because in the series you founded, scholars have translated 100 volumes of commentaries on Aristotle by ancient philosophers, many of whom were interested in the universe.

RS: It is true, to take an example, that there was a very interesting debate about the universe among the sixth century CE Greek philosophers commenting on Aristotle in Alexandria in Egypt, which was passed on to other cultures. There had by then been 600 years of commentary by Greek philosophers on Aristotle. But these late ones were the ones passed on from Alexandria to contemporary Christian monks in Syria speaking Syriac. Then, from the eighth century onwards, the caliphs of Baghdad brought in Syrian Christians, as well as Muslims, to translate Greek philosophy for people speaking Arabic in Baghdad, many of them Muslims, but some Christians. It was an enviably cosmopolitan period in philosophy. The debate about the universe was known quite early in Baghdad. It was about whether the universe had a beginning. Aristotle had said that the universe had no beginning and would have no end. In Plato, it was more ambiguous. Plato describes a Creator-God and it very much looks to the ordinary reader as if he is saying that God took beginningless matter and out of it created the ordered universe, as we know it, with a beginning. Moreover, through God's good will, it won't come to an end. However, that was not how Platonists read Plato later on. Why not? Partly because Aristotle severely attacked his teacher, Plato, on this issue of the orderly universe having had a beginning. Aristotle argued it was beginningless. It was partly to free Plato from Aristotle's objections that Platonists began to say Plato never intended to say that the universe had a beginning. Plato's Creator-God had beginninglessly produced a beginningless orderly universe. That reinterpretation of Plato made him agree with Aristotle that the orderly universe had no beginning. But there was a Christian pupil, Philoponus, of the leading Platonist in the sixth-century Alexandria. Steeped in more than 1,000 years of pagan Greek philosophy, Philoponus knew that the Platonists had accepted from Aristotle that there cannot be a more-than-finite number of anything; much less can infinity be increased, for one infinity cannot be larger than another. Aristotle's conception of infinity was one that is often taught in schools to this day, and defines infinity in terms of the finite, so that it looks less alarming. To talk of infinity, on this view, is to say that however large a *finite* number you have, there can always be a larger *finite* number. This works very well in application to the future. Starting from now, or from any date, and thinking into the future, if there will be an infinity of years, we will never reach a more-than-finite number of them. Rather, they will be infinite in Aristotle's sense, that however large a finite number of years has passed, a larger finite number will pass. But Philoponus asked about the *past*. If pagan Greek philosophers are right that the universe had no beginning, how many years will have passed up till now? A more-than-finite number. And how many days? More than that first infinity. But on their view of infinity, that should be impossible. So on their own terms, pagans should admit that Christianity is right: The universe had a beginning.

Philoponus was the odd man out among philosophers in Alexandria. But once translated into Arabic later in Baghdad, he was much more widely accepted. A number of Arabic-writing Christian philosophers preferred him. But Muslim philosophers in that open-minded society enjoyed the freedom to take either side. A number of them preferred Aristotle's beginningless universe, even though it fitted less well with Muslim theological doctrine on Creation. At the same time, they interpreted Philoponus as agreeing with Aristotle on many issues, and so were able to use him quite extensively. They further defended Aristotle, explaining why he had denied more-than-finite spatial entities, yet seems to have committed himself without comment to a more-than-finite past time. Any alleged infinite spatial entities could be moved side by side, or one on top of the other, and you would see the agreed absurdity of one being larger than the other. But times cannot be moved in this way.

Almost no Greeks challenged Aristotle's denial that one infinity can be larger than another, except for the mathematician Archimedes, who seems to have used that assumption in his geometry. The denial also seems to have been challenged by an early mathematician–philosopher writing in Arabic, Thabit ibn Qurrâ (d. 901), who commented on Archimedes. But a *philosophical* explanation of the sense in which one infinity can be larger than another, and the sense in which it cannot, may have had to wait until the Latin writers of the fourteenth century. Several of them offered a thought experiment that involved moving infinite series, but only in the imagination. Their argument might be put as follows: Take the infinity of years up till *now* and imagine it stretching away from your left eye. Then take the infinity of years up till the *next* year and imagine it stretching away from your right eye. Match the years in the two columns one-to-one, with the *present* year in one column aligned with the *next* year in the other. Neither column of years is larger than the other in the sense of 'sticking out beyond (*ultra* in Latin) the far end of the other', because neither column has an end. But the column which includes the *next* year is larger in that it includes all the same years as the other column, but it alone includes one 'besides' (*praeter*). 'Beyond' and 'besides' explain the sense in which a greater size of infinity is or is not allowed.

RJ: What the 100 translated volumes show us is that if Aristotle didn't exist, maybe Christian philosophy and Arabic philosophy would have had another destiny.

RS: You are right. Arabic philosophy was extremely original. It was as original as the Greek. But it was part of a conversation. If it hadn't been for the Greeks who inspired them, they wouldn't have had something to react to, or against, and to go beyond, and philosophy often depends on conversation. The first Greeks admittedly started without prior philosophy. But since then all of us have created on the basis of past conversation. We ignore past conversations at our peril. They expand our imaginations.

RJ: This has been a monumental work. How many years did it take for you to edit 100 volumes?

RS: I have been generously funded by many foundations since 1985, so that is 30 years, and I am still being funded by one of them, the Leventis Foundation. But the enterprise took the support of 72 translators, and altogether so far over 280 people in over 20 countries. So it has been very much a collective enterprise.

Part IV

Reading Ancient Greeks Today

Starting with Aristotle

RJ: Let us start with Aristotle because he occupies a very special space in your philosophical work. Is there a reason why you have concentrated many of your articles and books on Aristotle and not Plato or Socrates?

RS: Well, Aristotle was my first love, and I think it's a question of temperament. Of course, these two philosophers, teacher and pupil, are complementary to each other. Plato was not only a philosopher, but also a dramatic artist of great imaginative brilliance. Famously, he celebrated *Platonic* erotic love between mentor and protégé, and explained it by telling the story that the mentor's falling in love is due to our disembodied souls having once seen the Form of Beauty, when they processed around the edge of the physical universe in between reincarnations. He compares the rational, the domineering, and the appetitive elements of the soul to a charioteer (reason) and two horses. The soul, as it processes, may catch a glimpse of the Form of Beauty. But it does not retain a clear memory of it. Nonetheless, the sight of a beautiful youth reminds the soul unconsciously of the Beauty it has seen. This dramatic account has subsequently been applied to other forms of erotic love and has raised many philosophical questions. Aristotle was just the opposite. He learnt from Plato the basis of all his philosophical interests, but he likes to get everything he says sewn up, very crisp, with cross-references to definitions supplied by him elsewhere. His was a very different temperament, and philosophy needs both imagination and precision. But my temperament inclined me to getting things sewn up as far as I could. In the last 40 years, while retaining Aristotle, I have moved beyond him to new enthusiasms, but he was my starting place.

RJ: When did you start reading Aristotle? Was it when you were a student at Oxford? Who introduced you to Aristotle?

RS: Yes, when I was a student at Oxford. We had to be quite good at Greek and Latin. I studied Latin from the age of eight and Greek from the age of 11, and for the first two years at Oxford, I continued with just Greek and Latin, waiting till the last two years before I could study philosophy. Since I then specialized in ancient Greek philosophy, we read two books of ancient Greek philosophy, so I only read one book of Aristotle as an undergraduate and that was his *Ethics* and one book of Plato, his *Republic*. It was only as a postgraduate that I started to read the whole of Aristotle.

RJ: Who taught you Aristotle's *Ethics*? Was it one of the specialists of Aristotelian philosophy?

RS: Well, I had two opposite experiences because as an undergraduate student I had a wonderful teacher of Greek and Latin. He was a great friend and often came to my mother's house (she lived in Oxford) and he was very good to me. For philosophy, to which I was so much looking forward, my teacher had unfortunately not kept up with the subject. This would not be tolerated by the university nowadays, but I am talking about a long time ago. He never told me anything during the tutorials. He set me the same subject to write about for the first eight weeks running, and the same few things to read that I had read in the first week. When I asked what else I could read, he would say, 'Read the books', evidently meaning, although I did not understand at the time, the two books of Plato and Aristotle that I was already reading. I asked very politely to have a change of tutor, avoiding any complaint. But the head of my college sent my letter to my teacher who wrote to me and declined to release me. All the other students he sent on to other teachers, but me he kept. So the only solution was to pay out of my own pocket and find postgraduate students to teach me philosophy. I used to read them an essay on Monday and would come to my official teacher and read him the same essay later in the week. He just asked me questions for information about the philosophical scene. He had not heard, or pretended not to have heard, of what was then the leading philosophy journal, and he asked me who was his Oxford colleague whose book I greatly admired, and who was later to hold the chair at Cambridge. He was said to have claimed that he would rather be a master of foxhounds than an Oxford tutor. He never said 'You're good', he never said 'You're bad'; so I assumed I was mediocre and when I had finished, I left.

RJ: So you discovered the Greek texts on your own?

RS: No, I was lucky that I chose a friend who was a postgraduate student, the same age as me, but since he hadn't spent time doing military service, he was a little ahead of me. He later became a permanent teacher at Oxford and gave me wonderful tutorials. His name was Michael Woods. He died early, but I was lucky to have him. When I left, I became an elementary school master at the school I had loved. I knew at the age of nine that I wanted to be a teacher, and I would have been very happy as any sort of teacher, with people who wanted to learn at any rate. I did enjoy my one year, but fortunately, my examiners who were independent from my teacher asked, 'Why aren't you coming back after your examinations?' And so I was overjoyed. When I returned, I had as teachers two of the three most brilliant people (in England) at ancient philosophy, one ebullient and one retiring, but both very kind. Both became friends, and I learnt a great deal. I have never lost my amazement that people went on to pay me a salary for what I wanted to do most.

RJ: Do you remember the first essay that you wrote on ancient philosophy?

RS: Well, that was on Aristotle's *Ethics* with my friend teaching me and so my essay was very elementary. But he taught me accuracy in reading a text, and I came to know some of Aristotle's books by heart. I didn't make any original discoveries. I suppose when I was a postgraduate student, perhaps at first on Aristotle's psychology, I began to make some discoveries, and later one of my two professors did commission me to write a book. Actually, the book I wrote became too large for his series and expanded into something else. Besides Aristotle's psychology, I was very keen at that time on Aristotle's account of the physical universe on which I came to write later.

The Concept of Memory

RJ: One of your first books is on the concept of memory in Aristotle's philosophy.

RS: Yes, because I started with psychology. One of my two professors, the retiring one, who was wonderfully accurate, commissioned me to do a translation with notes on Aristotle's treatises on memory and sense perception. But when it grew too big for his series, I took the risk of submitting it to a different publisher, on condition that they produced a paperback edition. The publisher accepted the book, but said, of course, they couldn't do a paperback. So I took another risk and took the book away. It was then that I was lucky enough to be introduced to a wonderful publisher and classical scholar, Colin Haycraft, the head of Duckworth Publishers.

RJ: In your book, you mention that Aristotle's account of memory is fuller than that of the best-known British empiricists. If this is the case, why is his contribution so underestimated by contemporary psychologists?

RS: One way in which Aristotle anticipated the British empiricists is that he discusses how to remind yourself of things. So he invented something which 2,000 years later was much loved by the British empiricists—the theory of association of ideas. Your ideas, he said, are connected in chains by the three relations of similarity, contiguity, or opposition between the things you are trying to remember. If you want to remember where you left your keys, you think of the places where you have been, and one of those places will be contiguous to where you left your keys. If you are trying to remember one person, you will think of a similar person. Aristotle also discussed an already existing system of memorization, called the place system, which came to be used very much in the Middle Ages as well as in antiquity. If you want to memorize the names of the students in your classroom, you can memorize up to 200 names. But someone in antiquity, Seneca's father, claimed that he had been able to memorize 2,000 names after a single hearing. If one of your students is called Robinson, you form an image of a robin and his little son and then for Smith you form the image of a blacksmith. But that is not all, because you have to remember the names in the right order, you also prepare your mind in advance by pre-memorizing a street of houses, or other set of consecutive *places*. The houses memorized should be very distinctive, and if Robinson is the first person to remember, your imagination stations the robin and his son outside House No. 1 in the street. When explaining the system, Aristotle uses letters of the alphabet to show which places in the sequence he is referring to. If you are seeking one item in the sequence, start by looking at Image A. If that image does not match what you want, skip to Image C and take a quick look on either side. If that fails, skip to F and again take a quick look on either side. The scribes who copied Aristotle's text were completely baffled, and so all the letters got scrambled. I discovered what the original letters were by corresponding with a wonderful Soviet neuroscientist, A.R. Luria, who had a patient whose memory was defective but extraordinary, in that he had brilliant visual imagery. He could remember anything he wrote on the blackboard 30 years ago. If things had been misspelt or written badly, he might misread them when consulting the imagery he had retained, but he would not misremember how they looked. It was a great handicap for life to have such a memory, but it meant that he could perform memory feats. The important thing for me was that he reinvented for himself the place system all over again. I wrote to Luria and discovered that neither of them knew that the place system of memory was an ancient and medieval one. From his description of how he reinvented the place system, I saw exactly what letters needed restoring in Aristotle's scrambled text.

RJ: Aristotle uses the word 'remembering', but is this act of remembering only a mental image? Or does it also include judgment and intelligence?

RS: He liked to separate sense perception strongly from reason and intellect. As a biologist, he liked to classify animals as different from humans in not being able to reason. This doesn't mean that they are not intelligent, because he gave enormous power to perception. He says the lion perceives that the ox is near and rejoices that he will have a meal. There's emotion, there's perception, and the lion's perception has a very full content: that the ox is near. But unlike deliberate recollection by place memory, he doesn't think that it involves reason. Of course, humans can use reason in addition when they are perceiving or remembering. But he says that mental imagery, even that used in geometry, is a function of perception, not of reason, because mental images are wholly derived from sense perception, even though doing geometry is, of course, thinking and reasoning.

RJ: How come memory belongs to animals if they lack intelligence and judgment?

RS: They have intelligence, not judgment. The lion's perceiving that the ox is near involves perceiving *that* something is the case; it involves connecting the ox with a nearby position, it involves combining these ideas. But perception can do this. Memory can do the same. You can remember that the ox had been near. But neither perceiving nor memory is, for Aristotle, judging.

RJ: But do animals have a memory of the past?

RS: Yes, a very good memory.

RJ: Is it a memory of the past, or a perception of the present?

RS: It is a memory of the past due to the retention of the earlier perceptual data in the form of images. Aristotle's view of perception is different from Plato's, who whittled down perception to just perception of colours, flavours, and so on. He allowed no perception that something *is* the case. For Plato, that would be the work of reason and opinion, so this is a big difference from Aristotle.

Sense Perception in Greek Philosophy

RJ: In your article on Aristotle's theory of sense perception, you mention that Aristotle gives to perceptual content one of the most massive expansions in the history of Greek philosophy.

RS: Yes, that's true.

RJ: So it means that his work on perception was very innovative?

RS: It was a deliberate departure from Plato, motivated by his interest in trying to get a biological classification. Only humans have reason, all animals have sense perception and desire. Plants only have the ability to preserve their structure through nutrition and reproduce. He was aware that it was very difficult to classify borderlines, that between plants and sponges, for example.

RJ: I go back to my initial question. Why don't the contemporary psychologists read Aristotle anymore?

RS: If you answer an advertisement in the press about improving your memory, you will be sold what is in fact the Aristotle's system of place memory. Nonetheless, memorization was in Aristotle's day more important than it is now to the most successful careers, because it was necessary for becoming a good orator and hence a good lawyer or a good politician. These were the most prominent professions, although Aristotle used memorizing instead for training students in philosophical argument, not for oratory. But nowadays, we don't memorize much. We possess printed books, which are easy to produce in quantity, and electronic books; we have television, and electronic messaging instruments of ever-changing sorts, none of which require memory. On the other hand, we are very interested in psychotherapy, and the people who really invented what is nowadays called cognitive therapy were the Stoics, who were Aristotle's rivals and who started 22 years after his death, in the same city of Athens.

RJ: Do you believe that the new technologies are actually discouraging the new generations from reading the Greeks and the Romans?

RS: Oh, no, not at all. Computing has produced unimaginable aids to scholarship about the past. Moreover, people are tremendously interested, for example, in the psychology of the ancient Stoics. This week was the world Stoic Week. I spoke in the London celebration, but it was going on in Bangalore and all over the world, and I was amazed. I worked on the Stoic theories in the 1990s, when fewer people were working on them. But now I was asked to speak to 250 people from all walks of life, not just students or academics, who were so well-informed about the Stoics, and not only about the Stoics but also about the Bhagavadgita and Buddhism. So many people have learnt that these are the guides to life. But people read Aristotle for a different purpose. We were only talking about his psychology. But many people think that Aristotle got ethics right. Several things they like very much. He concentrates not on the rules of conduct which have had a dominant role in the last 200 years of Western ethics, but on your character. Character is what is important, and your character depends on having the right idea of what is important in life. Given those priorities, it may not be very useful to formulate the rules of conduct. On Aristotle's view, you have instead to be perceptive about the important things in very particular situations. He was a particularist. He also thought that there is not just one value, or a few, and I think he's right about that. There are many values, even more than the Stoics recognized. He was far removed from the view that only one thing matters. No, lots of things matter. So, many people like his ethics.

Return to the Stoics

RJ: I understand the general interest in the Stoics. I think since our world is going through a spiritual crisis, people think that reading Epictetus or Marcus Aurelius is a kind of spiritual exercise, but in the case of Aristotle, reading his writings on politics and ethics would teach us a lot more on how to govern our world today.

RS: Aristotle had a rather exclusive outlook, and so his politics may have less appeal in democratic societies. He thought that only a few people could attain a really worthwhile life. They would have had to be brought up well; they should spend their leisure in the right way. Contrary to Plato again, he considered the theatre played an important role in regulating emotions. The theatre would be available to everybody in Athens. But he thought that above all a truly worthwhile life included philosophy. Philosophy required leisure, which in turn required wealth or wealthy friends (Aristotle himself was a foreigner in Athens). Very few people have the opportunity for all of that. It was an exclusive recipe. He did discuss what to do if you lived in a city that didn't encourage this kind of life—he was very practical. But until 200 years after his death, the main philosophy schools tended to talk about the ideal person, and this too is a little off-putting, because few of us have any hope of being ideal.

This last piece of exclusivism was changed by one of the later Stoics, who headed the Stoic school in Athens around 129–109 BCE, Panaetius. He said that we don't live among ideal people; we live among ordinary people who are imperfect, so let's think about them. This, I think, made an important change, because then the Stoics talked above all about ordinary people with their failures and foibles and how they could progress in the right direction. Certainly, they all talked about progress before, but there was something depressing about what they said. Ideal people were exceedingly rare, perhaps there had been none, and they added something even more depressing. They said that until you are ideal, you are absolutely vicious. A person who is six feet under the water may have made progress towards the surface, but is as unable to breathe as someone who is 100 feet under the water. Panaetius instead spoke of degrees of virtue, so progress could take the form of getting a bit more of virtue as you progress. By taking into account the ordinary person, the later Stoics really tap you on the shoulder. They know your weaknesses and advise you on what to do about them. Nobody can escape; nobody can say they don't have these faults or weaknesses. It doesn't matter that this is the twenty-first century; our weaknesses are the same. The Stoics were appreciated by the Christians. Three copies of Epictetus have been found in Christian monasteries, which were used for training monks. The teachings of the Stoic emperor Marcus Aurelius were also much admired by Christians for very good reasons.

RJ: So when you say that Aristotle talks about a life of excellence, is he only thinking of a privileged group, or is he saying that anyone can think of having a life of excellence?

RS: No, that was a Stoic view. Of the two great Stoics I have mentioned, Epictetus was an ex-slave; he was also exiled from Rome by the emperor. The other Stoic, Marcus Aurelius, was himself the emperor. At either extreme you could be a Stoic.

Living with Excellence

RJ: Excellence is one of the concepts which is terribly missing in our world. So I think that by going back to the Stoics, we can deploy a new idea of excellence. I am sure that many people around the world think that excellence is something which is completely missing in their lives.

RS: There are many different forms of excellence, and some are difficult or actually impossible to combine. In our discussion of Gandhi, I argued that it is impossible to practise love of all humans, as he did, and also give due attention to your close family. There are other excellences that are difficult to combine, though some people succeed in combining them. The head of an organization should understand sympathetically the needs of the people for whom they are responsible. But they also need a sharp elbow, to remind troublemakers that there is a limit not to be overstepped. It is rare but admirable to be able to combine these excellences. Aristotle was particularly aware that there are many different forms of excellence. But I am going away from a Greek tradition when I say that because there isn't only one form of excellence, it would mislead people to say there's such a thing as excellence and they should approach it. It is better to think that there are some things we aren't going to be good at, but we should try to be good at some and improve on others, because we can't be good at all. This is opposite to a view found in Socrates as presented by Plato, in Aristotle, and in the Stoics, that the excellences, or rather the moral excellences, are inseparable, so that if you have one, you will have them all. This view tends to be arrived at by basing moral excellence on a very comprehensive form of understanding. To understand properly what one moral excellence calls for, you must understand the claims of the other moral excellences, so that your decisions take into account all the excellences correctly weighted. I doubt if such an ability is to be found in humans.

RJ: From what I know, Aristotle and the Stoics do not distinguish between private excellence and public excellence. There is no such thing as a private excellence, excellence in the home, *oikos*.

RS: I think Aristotle is different on that, because he discusses in *Nicomachean Ethics* (8.12) and *Politics* (3.4) the roles of husbands and wives in the domestic economy. The man's role is to acquire, the woman's to preserve. Thus, they supply each other with their own contributions to their common good. From this, not only is utility gained, but also pleasure, and if they have the different excellences appropriate to men and women, their friendship will be of Aristotle's highest kind, based on excellence. This is not our present view of the roles of women. It is also very different from Plato's idea in his *Republic*, that some women are so intelligent that they could become philosopher queens in the ideal society, but that most women are good only at weaving and watching pots. Women philosophers are accommodated in three of the four dominant philosophy schools I have mentioned: those of the Platonists, Stoics, and Epicureans. My impression is that women philosophers are less mentioned as members of the Aristotelian school. If so, it would be worth considering whether this is because of Aristotle's separation of roles.

Being a Stoic Today

RJ: Is it possible to be a Stoic today?

RS: Very much so, but a selective Stoic, borrowing from some of their insights, not endorsing the whole system. One valuable thing is Panaetius's advice on how to make decisions in life, which requires you to ask who you are in particular and to recognize that rules need to take account of particular facts, not only of universal ones. Should you show family loyalty and follow your father's career? He was a successful lawyer. But you must ask what your personal talents are or could be. Would you make a good lawyer, or would you let your father down? The right decision depends on who you are. There might be a decision that would be right for you, but for nobody else at all. Cicero illustrates Panaetius's point by the example of the younger Cato. When Julius Caesar was bringing an end to the Roman Republic in his quest for personal power, he advanced on the city of Utica. It was then right for the younger Cato, who was in the city, to commit suicide rather than parley with Caesar. But it would not have been right *for anyone else in the same circumstances*. Why not? Because Cato was unique in the way he had stood all his life for uncompromising rectitude and for the Roman Republic. This is very different from Kant's search for universal rules, and Kant's student who recorded Kant referring to the point about Cato clearly did not understand it.

Different again was Epictetus's question that we discussed in our earlier talk, the one about selfhood. He asked about freedom; have we not all enslaved ourselves to something? Just when you were congratulating yourself that you did not share other people's enslavements, Epictetus found yours. Have you enslaved yourself to books? In this age, it may be on your computer or other preferred electronic device that you do your reading and writing. Have you enslaved yourself to that device? How do you react when it is not working?

The Stoics were extraordinarily good at spotting what your problems would be in life 2,000 years later. When I was told by my doctor to do more exercise, I wondered what would be the right exercise for a philosopher. Not going to a gym, which would remove two hours from study every day. I finally settled on brisk walking. Then I found that Seneca's *Letters from a Stoic* had addressed exactly this question: what is the right physical exercise for a philosopher? He too had ruled out weightlifting, running, and had got down to walking. But he went one better than me. The best exercise for a philosopher is being carried in a litter. It exercises every muscle in your body as you are bumped up and down—as I knew from Cornelia Sorabji, who had been carried that way through the jungles of India. But Seneca had an extra comment: You can continue dictating your thoughts to your secretary who will be running alongside.

Again of value was the Stoic idea that you should extend the good feelings which it would be natural for you to have for your own physical person and for your closest family to your more distant family, then to your fellow citizens, to foreigners, including eventually all humans. The Stoics thought that accorded with nature, not that it was easy. They saw these degrees of affection for fellow humans as so many concentric circles surrounding your mind at the centre, with your body as the first circle around it, then the closest relatives, and so on. They did not imagine that you could feel as close to the distant as you do to the near. But they did recommend that you pull each circle inwards to make it closer to the next one in. As so often, they gave exercises to help you. It matters what you call people. In India, many women are called *Auntie*. The Bengali systems of family names are completely different from the English ones. If you call cousins 'brothers', would you not tend to feel more obligations to them, and fewer obligations if you had no easy name for other relations? The Stoics advise you to give to relatives further out the names used for those at the next level in. Gandhi, we saw in our second talk, practised a certain kind of love for all humans, although in order to do so, he reversed what the Stoics thought natural, and recommended putting the family last. Christ qualified the commandment of the Hebrew Old Testament, 'Thou shalt love thy neighbour as thyself', by rejecting the interpretation that you shall hate your enemy (Matthew 5.43–8). Love confined to those who love you, he said, was practised even by the disliked tax collectors of his time.

We earlier discussed Epictetus's idea of freedom as invulnerability as something practised by Gandhi. That is a practice for heroes. But even the unheroic have something to learn from Epictetus's idea that what overcomes your better wishes is not someone else, but another wish of yours, a wish to comply. Only the hero will adopt this policy at the risk of life, limb, or liberty. But it can help the unheroic to remember that if you follow the popular line of conduct, it is only by your wish. Good administrators may have to risk failure by standing up for something unpopular.

Especially important is the Stoic invention of cognitive therapy, not for avoiding emotion generally, as they wished, but for avoiding unwanted and unproductive emotions. Their advice on how to avoid unnecessary anger, or unnecessary depression at the everyday ups and downs of life, is of the greatest value. And the most famous of the early Stoics, Chrysippus, said he could teach the therapy to those who weren't Stoics, so he allowed for those who did not accept the whole system. I would not want to accept their advice on how to avoid sorrow altogether. In order to avoid sorrow at bereavement, one would have had to lead a rather detached family life, I believe.

RJ: But if one is a believer, he or she believes in life after death.

RS: Neither the Stoics, nor Aristotle, nor the Epicureans believed in life after death. Out of the four schools I have emphasized, only Plato's did. The Stoics thought a soul which had enough physical tension might avoid dispersal for a short while after death. But they did not regard their belief in the exact repetition of history an infinite number of times as giving you any kind of immortality.

RJ: Are you saying that anyone who believes in life after death cannot be a Stoic and cannot have the Stoic consolation about suffering in life?

RS: No, they won't be Stoic, although they can borrow the Stoic consolations. But belief in life after death is also a consolation, and so is belief in a God so benevolent to each individual that, as the Christian New Testament says, he has numbered every hair of your head. I think people who believe in this are lucky. I have seen this belief acting as a source of strength in lives that were very difficult. But, of course, such beliefs can also be misused in any religion that entertains them, as a source of threat, to emphasize hell, and to give undue importance to priests as the only human channel for salvation. This is not the attitude of any priests I know, but it has historically been a complaint in disputes, for example, between the Protestant and Catholic Christians in the sixteenth century. For those who don't have such a belief, I think the Stoics can offer a great deal of help for everyday life.

I don't, however, recommend the Stoic methods of avoiding distress at the great tragedies of life, as I said in our earlier talk about the case of bereavement. The advice of Epictetus is, when kissing your wife, to say to yourself you are kissing a mortal. This might create a greater sense of value in old age, but it would be a rather detached attitude in youth.

Ashoka and Marcus Aurelius

RJ: Well, I'm thinking that people who are reading our book might ask this question, especially about Marcus Aurelius as an emperor: How can you be an emperor and not have lust for power? And maybe there is a comparison to make with Ashoka, who became a Buddhist—how can you be a Buddhist and an emperor at the same time? How can you be a Stoic and an emperor at the same time?

RS: That is a very interesting question. Marcus Aurelius was unusual, because as emperor he kept a private diary, which he did not intend to publish, of reminders to himself of how to remain a Stoic under tremendous provocation. It was published as *Meditations* quite some time after his death; he didn't intend it. From it you see what he felt were his weaknesses, such as losing his temper sometimes. But it's very impressive because, as we discussed previously, he says to himself: 'These people are plotting against me, but that's what they think would be best. Just understand that they can't think otherwise.' No anger is expressed. Unlike Ashoka's public inscriptions, Marcus was writing private *Meditations*.

RJ: I am always very much intrigued by the fact that among the Stoics, you have philosophers who are directly influenced and interested by politics. Seneca is also very much *involved in* everyday politics. But they practise at the same time a kind of ethical philosophy, which is quite astonishing.

RS: Seneca was tutor to the terrible tyrant Nero, and got rather compromised over the cover-up of Nero's murder of his own mother, but at the end he died a courageous death on Nero's orders. Other Stoic aristocrats opposed the emperors outright. They all needed Stoic ethics in order to stand up in this way. But even nowadays politicians could benefit from Stoic ethics, for example, on how to deal with the loss of office. When Mrs Thatcher was our prime minister, her committees used to ask academics questions about the relevance of their work. It would have been very relevant to the loss of office, which, for all her talents, she found difficult to cope with. She herself mentioned the Stoics once, to deflate the French as having been anticipated by the British Magna Carta and in the invention of human rights, an invention to which they were laying claim. I wrote a piece disagreeing with that interpretation of the Stoics, and no doubt others could have done so on Magna Carta. But at least she recognized the Stoics as having contributed to ideas about justice which were relevant to politics.

RJ: Do you think that people like Havel or Mandela had this capacity to cope with the loss of office?

RS: Perhaps they had the ability for other reasons. But the Stoics can help you crystallize your tendencies, and be on the watch for ways of reinforcing them.

Aristotle on Self-Awareness

RJ: Could we go back to Aristotle? Let us now take up the question of perception and its relation with self-awareness. In your study on Aristotle's perceptional functions, you underline the fact that ancient texts discuss the need for a unitary subject of awareness. Is the notion of self-awareness essential for the ancients as much as it is for the moderns?

RS: Yes, they were very interested in self-awareness. Aristotle thought it was one of the values of friendship, that it helps you to be aware of yourself, because the friend is another self, and you can learn by seeing in your friend both virtues and shortcomings as if you were looking in a mirror. But they didn't all agree on whether you know yourself best through a friend, or whether you know yourself best directly. It was Plato who first suggested that another person can be a mirror, but not everybody accepted that, and some of the later followers of Plato, the ones we call Neoplatonists, thought you had *direct* knowledge of yourself. Plato himself, who was always so imaginative, raised problems about whether one could ever have knowledge about one's self, whether the idea of self-knowledge was, for some reason, impossible. But there were also later Platonists who thought self-knowledge is guaranteed; you could hardly fail to know what is going on in your own mind.

You asked me in particular about a unitary subject of self-awareness. That question of unity of awareness was taken forward by Aristotle, but in response to a question of his teacher, Plato: How do we compare and distinguish sweet and white and tell that something *is* sweet and white. Sameness, difference, and being, Plato thought, must go beyond the work of sight and taste, and must call for reason and belief. But Aristotle gave perception a wider role. He said that *perception* can perceive that sweet is different from white, but it must do so by means of a single thing. It cannot perceive the difference by taste alone, nor by vision alone. It must perceive it by some general perceptual faculty which bridges the five senses. Otherwise, it would be as if *you* perceive sweet and *I* perceive white, and no comparison would be made. Very much later, certain Neoplatonists went further: We don't just have perceptions of sweet and white; we are also aware of our perceptions, and not only of our perceptions, but also of our *desires* of different kinds and of *cognitions* of different kinds—thoughts and reasonings. So once again, we need a *unitary* faculty that gives us awareness of *all* of these: our perceptions, desires, and thoughts. One of them, therefore, in the sixth century CE postulated a general faculty of *attention*, meaning attention to self, the *prosektikon*, to be aware of all our psychological activities. That was an advance, but I think that unity is best found in another direction: There is somebody who *owns* or *has* all of these things—the perceptions, desires, and thoughts—and owns the awareness of them all. The same owner, rather than the same faculty, gives us the unity, and I think the same owner constitutes a self.

Sharing Knowledge with Oneself

RJ: To continue with the idea of self-awareness, in your work on the Neoplatonists you mention that for them intellect is self-aware when it turns *in* on itself. We can see here a difference with Aristotle.

RS: The Neoplatonist view you just mentioned did start earlier than the idea of an attentive faculty. It is not a view I find philosophically persuasive, but it holds that thinking involves no physiology. Aristotle disagreed. But if there is none, the Neoplatonists thought, that is why thought can turn in on itself and penetrate itself, as bodies cannot. By contrast, perception requires physiology, and so awareness of perception is not through its turning in on itself. Rather, you are aware of perception through the mirror of imagination.

RJ: What is the difference between self-awareness and what some of the ancients called *suneidêsis*, sharing knowledge with oneself?

RS: It was a special use of this word which meant sharing knowledge with oneself. The special use started with the fifth century BCE playwrights in Athens, five centuries before Christ in Athens. If you have the full expression 'to share knowledge *with oneself*', what follows is practically always a defect, and it's the origin of the idea of bad conscience. You find it after the playwrights, in the fourth century in Plato. By the third and second centuries, it is in some of the earliest Latin comic playwrights. An important development was that people started talking about sharing knowledge with oneself not only of bad things in the past, bad conscience, but also of what it *would* be wrong to do in the future. The reference was nearly always to the knowledge of moral defects, although Plato has some examples of intellectual ones. The Greek phrase was picked up by Christians, initially by St Paul, who added some important points and the idea has lasted for 2,500 years, providing, I think, the core of the concept of conscience in Christianity, although there were variations, and sometimes deliberate violations. Where the Greek does not specify 'with oneself', there is a much wider range of meanings which can be distinguished only from the context.

RJ: This Greek idea of sharing knowledge with oneself also means sharing knowledge with others.

RS: When the qualification 'with oneself' is used, and we are talking about knowledge of the past, there is a guilty secret, which may be known by witnesses, confidants, or accomplices, and there may be a fear that it is known by others or by God. But the wish is to keep it secret, with only *oneself* sharing one's guilty knowledge, and not to share it with others more than necessary.

RJ: Oh, I see. So, there is a difference here with the Christian concept of 'conscience'. As you know, the concept of 'conscience' is central in Christian philosophy and later in modern philosophy.

RS: The Greek is not different from the Christian. When people are asked in Christianity to confess, the idea of a secret is still present. It is different, of course, when we are talking about possible *future* wrongdoing, and keeping a clear conscience. Then people may be talking *publicly* about avoidance, before there is any guilty secret to hide.

RJ: How much are we really aware today that we got the concept of 'conscience' from the Greeks and the Romans?

RS: I don't think people are very aware, because the first 500 years haven't been fully mapped out. But there is a great continuity. St Paul made one or two important additions. For one thing, he said, mercifully, that conscience is fallible. It would have been intolerable if people had gone around thinking otherwise. And he also drew a distinction between the moral law, which he thought was written by God in our hearts, the law of what would be wrong, and our fallible appeal to that law to defend ourselves. The different idea that conscience was God's voice was not St Paul's view. That idea does come in later, but it comes in first among Platonists as an interpretation of the view Plato ascribes to Socrates, that he had a guardian spirit, whose voice, Plato's very word, warned him against courses of action, when he was otherwise minded to take them, and whom Socrates treated as indubitable. Paul's view is mercifully different from that, since it recognizes our fallibility, and some of the greatest earlier Christians added that we may fail to read, or may misread, the law written in our hearts, so fallibility was accepted. At the beginning, among the early playwrights and Plato, the concept did not rely on the law of God, but was, to some extent, secular. It was argued increasingly by the eighteenth century that our values come from those who bring us up, rather than from God, and there has been important discussion since of how to make it less fallible. If the concept of conscience has been re-secularized, that does not diminish its value. It is a concept of what it was or would be wrong to do, and it is up to each person to think it out further in interaction with others.

Part V
War and Ethics

Going to War

RJ: Your book on the ethics of war that you edited with David Rodin is an important volume on a very urgent subject, which is on the question of just war. Were you motivated by the American invasion of Iraq and Afghanistan in 2003?

RS: Yes, I was. There was a lot of talk about just war at the time, which I hadn't known about very much before. I had read one of the few papers then written about just war by a modern English philosopher. But otherwise, I hadn't thought much about it. It began to be mentioned when there was discussion about the Iraq War and I did join the march in London to protest against the war. It wasn't an angry protest in any way. It was just expressing opinion in a good-natured way. As to how many joined the march, claims varied, but the estimate I first heard suggested two million marchers. The official figure was one million, but I heard that one million opponents of the war had already reached Hyde Park, when the queue of marchers behind them stretched back the entire width of central London as far as Waterloo. It was estimated that 52 per cent of the country was against the invasion of Iraq. So I think people were very dismayed, I was very dismayed, that the war went ahead. An untrue claim was put about that Saddam Hussein in Iraq could launch missiles at Britain in 45 minutes. I was in the USA in Texas, when the news of the invasion broke. We saw the first bombs falling and I was appalled, because by every criterion this failed to be a just war. Just to take five criteria formulated in the medieval Christian tradition and widely acknowledged, there should be a just cause, reasonable attempts at resolution of the dispute should have been exhausted, the right authority should authorize the war, the war should not make things even worse than they were already, and the aim of the war should be achievable. I wrote over the preceding months to three members of the government, including the foreign secretary and the Chancellor of the Exchequer who controls expenditure. I received replies from the foreign secretary, which was very civil of him because he must have had a lot of letters, and I believe he was a thoroughly decent man, and certainly my local Member of Parliament replied very conscientiously. I gave them information that they probably didn't have from the American Academy of Arts and Sciences, which had estimated the cost in trillions of dollars—an estimate that was to prove just about right. The only improvement arising from our resulting failure has been the requirement that in future Parliament, as a whole, must be asked to endorse a war. Of course, it is difficult to decide when a war might be justified. I am not a pacifist; Gandhi wasn't a pacifist. I do not believe that the Second World War was wrong and there will be other such rare cases of the need to protect oneself or others by military means. But some of the wars in my lifetime have been, I think, what used to be called wars of vanity, the vanity of princes. Even if we don't have princes in democratic societies, it is the vanity of their successors. There's no point in accusing particular people, but it is a way of appearing powerful to use armour, if you have lots of it. I didn't really follow wars closely except for the Second World War, until the Korean and Malaysian wars in which, as I said earlier, I missed serving by one year.

RJ: Have you ever been to a war yourself?

RS: I was very fortunate that my two years of compulsory military training did not subsequently lead me into war. When I was 18, one of the things the country wanted was people who would be very fluent speakers of Russian, since Soviet Russia seemed to be the great threat. It is very sensible to prepare to understand your opponents. I learnt Russian for 21 months and it was fascinating. My teachers had all escaped from Soviet Russia in horrifying circumstances, and they told me what they had suffered. The extraordinary thing about learning a language intensively is that you come to appreciate the culture that goes with the language. We had to work very hard. If we failed any one of the fortnightly exams, we were thrown off the course. I came to appreciate and love talking with my teachers all day, as we got better. Of course, you haven't thought things out when you are young, and I was just lucky that I didn't have to use my knowledge in warfare.

RJ: Did you have military exercises in school?

RS: Well, even though in school I had military exercises, I didn't really understand what we were doing. I thought it was strange that when we had bayonet practice, we had to rush at a sandbag with a bayonet and we all had to shout. I thought it was really funny that we were shouting; I supposed it was to encourage us to run faster. I didn't actually realize that that was not the purpose, until a mere decade or two ago when I heard somebody talking about warfare in Homer and how you had to make yourself angry. I suddenly realized what a fool I was.

The shouting was a sort of play acting, to stir up anger or even hatred for the enemy. I didn't think of this at the time. I didn't particularly wish to hate anybody, but I thought in defence of your country, so recently nearly invaded, you might actually have to use a bayonet and run faster. To build up your courage, you might have to shout.

Patriotism and War

RJ: Everyone considers you to be very peaceful and amiable, humane, I would say (some people think humanists preach atheism). But in those days, would you have thought of killing people in the name of patriotism?

RS: I fear that I would. What would I think now? You have had so much more of these ugly experiences than I have, and I am hardly entitled to talk at all. But I can make the question vivid to myself by recalling the smoke bricks I told you about earlier, in connexion with the Second World War. My parents were given smoke bricks to light, to screen our family house, because a war machine with overwhelming superiority was waiting day by day to parachute into family streets and shoot at family homes, and it was thought it was known to the day when they would parachute. It is hard to imagine what it's like to think that family homes will be invaded by an overwhelming parachute force. In those circumstances, I would kill to protect my family as long as I could, if we were all going to be killed. Protecting the family, not rights of self-defence, would be in my mind. But self-defence has often been thought to be a legitimate exception to restrictions on killing. The very first case I know where it was presented as a plea, however, was a somewhat bogus one. It was in a speech by the Roman orator Cicero and he was making a rather unjustified case. He was defending Milo, somebody accused of murder, and he presented it as a case of self-defence. He said there is a natural law permitting killing in self-defence, since nobody suggested there was then an actual law.

Western Tradition of Ethics of War

RJ: In the Introduction of your book, *The Ethics of War*, you mention that the book is extremely relevant to the present wars. But I think it is a book which is also very relevant to other times, and especially to the avoidance of war in the future. In what way do you think that the other traditions of thought have been subject to an ethical reflection on war in the same way as the Western tradition?

RS: I think the Roman tradition and then the later tradition of the Latin-speaking Middle Ages were practised at thinking about justifications for going to war. But I must interject something first, that the justifiability of war wasn't the original Christian attitude. Originally, the Christians took up one of Christ's sayings, which was that if your enemy strikes you on the cheek, turn the other cheek; invite him to hit the other side as well. In the first few centuries, as long as the Christians were the underdogs, that was the Christian attitude. They took Christ's own view, and concluded that the Christians should not fight in the Roman army. If they did, they were in the wrong, and if they shed blood in doing so, they must undertake severe penance for many years. But all that changed when the emperor of the Roman world, Constantine, became a Christian. Constantine declared himself a Christian in 317 CE. He didn't declare the empire Christian. No, he did something better than that; he called for toleration of all religions. But from then on, the Christians were in the saddle, and then the Christian ban on military service began to disappear. The Christian thinker Augustine, writing either side of 400 CE, less than a century after Constantine, was therefore in a very different situation, and he introduced the idea that some wars were just and others were unjust. That idea was further developed by scholars of Canon or Church law in the twelfth century, Gratian being the most famous of them, and then by Thomas Aquinas, the greatest of all the Christian philosophers in the thirteenth century. It was what I had hoped would stop an obviously unjust war now, because so many people in positions of authority said that the war was unjust. Those who wrote against the war in my co-edited book included the Bishop of Oxford, who spoke against the war in the House of Lords, and the former head of the Ministry of Defence, who also believed in the criteria for just war. I no longer have much hope in the idea of just war, because I think governments don't listen to that sort of thing.

The reason why Cicero was able to say so much already about the rules for going to war is that the fetial code of ancient Rome had a remarkable rule of its own. Before you go to war with somebody, you must give them 30 days' notice to meet your terms. The terms may be very severe, but you must make an effort to settle the issue by means other than war. Something else is equally important: Besides the conditions on which it is just to go to war are the conditions by which you should be governed when you are already fighting the war. When is it allowed to shoot if there are civilians around? How are you allowed to treat prisoners? Are you ever allowed to kill prisoners? When you have conquered a city, is it just fine if you rape all the women and loot? No, and actually it was the very early Islamic thought which had a more complete set of rules about justice in a war already started. One problem with the rules of conduct within war is that leaders have often demonized the enemy, in order to justify going to war. Demonization is a very bad thing, and Augustine made a requirement of a charitable attitude to the enemy, but this is hard to square with persuading people to go to war in the first place. In addition, by the time you win, you have suffered losses, your mates have been killed, you haven't seen your family, and some soldiers are suffering post-traumatic stress. It does not help if fighters are recruited with the sole motive of escaping poverty, or co-opted from security firms without training.

Authority and War

RJ: Among the reasons that nations go to war are reasons of state. (Are those your original words?) This reminds me of the relation that Augustine makes between authority and war. Is this relation still very relevant in the conception of just war today?

RS: Very relevant in England. Recently, because of the Iraq War, a new law was brought in, that Britain may not go to war without consulting Parliament. And Parliament refused to bomb Syria recently, when there was no plan of achievable action, which is a practical as well as an ethical requirement for going to war. In an earlier decade when a smaller circle decided, Prime Minister Harold Wilson declined to send British troops to the Vietnam War. In the medieval arrangement that Shakespeare describes, the circle of decision-making was smaller still. The prince decided whether a war was just or not. The soldiers were not to trouble their heads about it and were not responsible if the war was unjust. Some of the earliest attempts in England to *resist* conscription to war on grounds of conscience were in the seventeenth century when John Lilburne from a group called the Levellers tried, unsuccessfully, to persuade Oliver Cromwell that freedom of conscience should allow refusal to fight against one's conscience. In the First World War, Prime Minister H.H. Asquith was anxious to avoid opposition to the war, and so for a year he used only volunteers. When manpower shortages finally forced him to conscript, he nonetheless set up tribunals which could exempt people, not only on religious grounds, but for other reasons of conscience, or even on grounds of a political belief that the state had no right to assign employment. Over 10,000 were exempted, and only those who refused to appeal to tribunals, or to accept their verdicts, suffered punishment.

RJ: It is interesting that this concept of authority and its conceptual outcome was put into question by people like Las Casas in the defence of the Indians of South America. We also have a thinker like Francisco de Vitoria who thinks in relation to international law. What is your point of view on these two thinkers and the relevance of their thoughts for today's issues?

RS: This was about the conquest by Spanish adventurers in the sixteenth century of the various American Indian peoples in South America. It wasn't a government conquest, but it was extremely lucrative. It is very impressive that for a whole year the war was stopped by King Charles V of Spain, who was also the Holy Roman Emperor, in other words, the religiously sanctioned emperor of many European countries. So the most powerful ruler in Europe stopped the war for a year, while his thinkers debated the rights and wrongs. These thinkers were very clever men. Sepulveda was in favour of the war and Las Casas was, on the other side, against the war. He in turn would have known the work of another Spanish scholar earlier in the century, Vitoria, who had also put very severe restrictions on war, based on his interpretation of Thomas Aquinas and the earlier tradition. Charles V would have had the authority to stop the war, but unfortunately his advisers reached no decision and it resumed.

The Stoics and War

RJ: We are talking about the law of nations, which was promoted by Vitoria. But why don't we find this notion of the law of nations in the Stoic philosophy despite the fact that there is the idea of attachment to one's fellow human beings?

RS: The Stoics did have the equivalent. It was Cicero in the first century BCE, not a Stoic but an approving reporter of the Stoics, who in his *On Duties* made the first reference I know to the law of nations (*ius gentium*). But he treated it as equivalent to the law of *nature* or natural law, which the Stoics spoke of and identified with reason. It was probably the Stoics who influenced Cicero, when he added that the true law received from nature is *internal* to us and is our reason. But the idea of natural law goes back to the Greeks earlier than the Stoics. It was first called divine law, as superior to human law, in the fifth century BCE by the pre-Socratic philosophers Heraclitus and Empedocles, and by the heroine of Sophocles's play *Antigone*. Aristotle, in the fourth century, reports the last two cases and adds a fourth century sophist and orator, Alcidamas, who even before the Stoic attack on the idea of natural slavery said that nature had made nobody a slave. Over 200 years after Cicero, the law of nations was distinguished from natural law and downgraded. Tony Honoré suggested that this was because in 212 CE Roman citizenship was extended to all nations throughout the empire, and so the law of nations could no longer be seen as a natural unwritten law distinct from, and superior to, the written laws applied to Roman citizens. The jurist Ulpian around this time repeats that all humans are by natural law born free and are guaranteed some modest rights. So the practice of freeing them can only be based on the inferior law of nations.

RJ: It seems to me that many modern philosophers were not in support of the Stoics' acceptance of natural law and the unity of mankind.

RS: Yes, the division of opinion started in antiquity, because the Epicureans and the Stoics represent very different standpoints on this matter, which have lasted till and influenced the present day. It concerns whether you think that the true human nature is nice or not, and what role nature plays. The Stoic view, as we've seen, was that nature calls on us to try to recognize our real affinity and try to feel some love towards all human beings, including foreigners and slaves. Their contemporaries in Athens, the Epicureans, said you can see that what humans and animals alike are seeking from birth is pleasure. But it took time for humans to discover what gives pleasure naturally. Competition does not. Eventually, because of their rationality, humans were able to discover that contracts not to harm or be harmed are what provide the natural guarantee of equanimity, which is what pleasure consists in. Without contracts that actually succeed in delivering the necessary security, there is no justice. Nature would not on its own encourage mutual affection, as the Stoics said, but allowed competitive insecurity. Nature plays the different role of determining what would actually be useful in providing the security and hence the tranquillity in which pleasure consists, and it took human rationality to discover this and to artificially introduce punishments and laws.

The great English proponent of this sort of view is Thomas Hobbes, who published in very interesting circumstances in the seventeenth-century England, at the time of civil wars, the execution of the king, and the temporary suspension of the monarchy. He started out as tutor to the heir of the throne and retreated with the royal family to France. He was already writing his great book *Leviathan* there, but when he published it in 1651, the king had already been executed in 1649. Hobbes was back in London, and the principal person in charge was Oliver Cromwell, who never accepted the crown, but who eventually did accept the title of Lord Protector. Hobbes published his view as a case for there being one all-powerful ruler; he did not present it as a case for kingship. I think Cromwell believed, as no doubt intended, that he himself fitted the picture. But it was awkward when the monarchy was restored in 1660 and those who had executed the king were themselves executed or disinterred and mutilated. Hobbes had to stress that the king fitted his call for rule by one man. The call was based on the need for a *contract* to gain security from what he called the state of *nature*. In that state, he said life was nasty, brutish, and short. This conception of the natural was even more opposed to Stoicism, because it seemed to make hostility, not amity, natural. To gain security from the power of the ruler, people must give up the mere opinions of their private consciences, which had been so much invoked by dissenters during the civil wars, and must follow public conscience, which was the ruler's law. The contract remained valid only for so long as the ruler did deliver the contracted security.

My own prejudice is for the Stoic view, and against the Epicurean, on this matter. The belief that other humans are naturally hostile is needlessly self-fulfilling, since people unsurprisingly react to such a hostile attitude. Moreover, no human can be trusted with such power over private consciences. Nonetheless, you can see that these are two very grand conceptions, each with adherents to this day, entrenched in two great camps.

Humanitarian Intervention in Ancient Times

RJ: Could we go back to the concept of just war? In democratic countries today we don't have the rule of one man, but we do have the concept of human rights which has a significant role to play in moral philosophy and in relation to what is these days called 'humanitarian intervention'. Humanitarian intervention argues in favour of military violence with the aim of protecting the rights of people. Did we have such a notion in ancient times?

RS: Human rights and humanitarian intervention both have interesting histories. I mentioned earlier about my disagreement with Margaret Thatcher's claim that the Stoics invented the idea of human rights. They invented the idea of justice for all humans, which was important enough. I argued that it was not the idea of human rights, because the focus was on virtue requiring you to meet the needs of other humans; whether those needs were successfully met was by comparison only a 'preferred indifferent'. The idea of human rights has been traced by Daniel Deckers to twelfth-century Canon lawyers and it reappears in the Spanish critic of the conquest of South America, Vitoria, in the sixteenth century, who was drawing on Thomas Aquinas's treatment of natural law. Attention has also been drawn to some minimal rights accorded to slaves on the basis of natural law as early as the third-century Roman jurist Ulpian. I think the idea of humanitarian intervention is also not new, but again I am thinking of a later time. The case I am remembering isn't ancient but once again comes in the sixteenth-century controversy in Spain. One of the excuses for going on with the conquest of the Indians in South America was that they engaged in human sacrifice and that we should be protecting the victims of sacrifice. To this, a very convincing answer was given: In the process, you will kill far more civilians than have ever been sacrificed. Very occasionally, it probably is possible to help others by military means without incurring this risk, but that needs much more careful thought than is usually given.

The Concept of Just War

RJ: We don't need to be pacifists to understand that what we call humanitarian intervention is a contradiction in terms. As a matter of fact, we can never have a full picture of the culture of a country, or the tragedy that is going on in that country. I think that the Indians knew that very well because when we read the Bhagavadgita, we see no comments on the justice of war.

RS: Very interesting. Nick Allen pointed out in the book on war that I co-edited that the Bhagavadgita does explicitly recognize the rules for justice *within* the conduct of war. But the justice of *going* to war appears to be taken for granted by Lord Krishna.

RJ: It is especially hard to balance the rights and wrongs on either side.

RS: Such problems may be why the Geneva Conventions focus, like the Bhagavadgita, on the rules of conduct *within* a war, and I suppose mutual fear may have a better chance of succeeding on some questions, such as the treatment by either side of prisoners. Rules about *going* to war may be harder to implement because going to war is too much in the hands of princes for whom the temptation is often too great.

RJ: Now most of the religious and moral traditions talk not only about just war, but also about peace. Peace is considered as the absence of war. Do we find an equivalent of Kant's *Perpetual Peace* among the Greek philosophers? Kant talks about the federation of republics because he wants to construct peace among different constitutional frameworks. This was not necessarily the case in the ancient times.

RS: I don't think we have an equivalent. Aristotle was particularly insistent that the whole purpose of war is peace. He also described in his *Politics* what type of constitution rendered the ubiquitous civil wars of his time less likely, namely, having a large enough economic middle class. But this falls short of a programme for perpetual peace. The Cynic Diogenes and the third head of the Stoics, Chrysippus, both wrote books echoing Plato's title of *Republic*, and both are recorded as having said that in the ideal republic armies would be useless. But how they would defend themselves from an external attack, even if everybody *within* the ideal republic was wise, is not recorded.

Moderation and Peace

RJ: Many philosophers in medieval times consider Aristotle as a philosopher of moderation. Averroes, who is an Aristotelian philosopher, thinks that there are times when peace is more reasonable than war. Is that because he is also a philosopher of moderation? In other words, does the concept of peace go hand in hand with the concept of moderation: moderation in politics, moderation in public life, and moderation as a form of excellence?

RS: Certainly. Noah Feldman describes in our co-edited book, *The Ethics of War*, Averroes's handling of the problem that in the Koran there are two verses that seem to advocate war against non-believers in Allah and polytheists (that would exclude Jews and Christians), against one verse in favour of accepting their suing for peace. Averroes treats this in two works. In one, his legal handbook, he simply records interpretations. Only in the other does he reveal his own view. One interpretation had been that the war verses were written later and superseded the peace verse, but that non-believers had a choice of ending the war by paying the poll tax instead of accepting conversion. The other interpretation was that the verses were compatible, since the peace verse allowed a cessation of war, if some necessity made it in the Muslims' interest, as judged by the relevant imam. In his other work, Feldman points out, Averroes discusses Aristotle's highly original account in his *Nicomachean Ethics* (5.7) of how a judge must be allowed to exercise discretion in order to practise equity. Averroes cites as his own example the Muslim law of war against their opponents. But since it may be impossible to uproot all opponents, peace may be more choice-worthy than war, and by not understanding this, the Muslim public can create great harm.

We might call Averroes moderate in the sense you have in mind, but his rationale here is not an appeal to moderation. Aristotle was explicitly described as advocating moderation, but in a different sense. He believed in moderation in emotion (*metriopatheia*). He also saw the virtues, including good temper, as hitting a midpoint or 'mean' between extremes. He recommended the right amount of anger, according to the circumstances and the demands of other virtues besides good temper. The Stoics disagreed. They believed in non-emotion (*apatheia*) through eradication, not moderation, of nearly all emotion. Their grounds were that most emotion involves wrong evaluation of what is good or bad and of what reaction is appropriate. But I am not sure that Aristotle's advocacy of moderation, or the Stoic rejection of it as insufficient, were connected particularly with the prevention of war. Aristotle's account of the virtue of courage assumes that courage will be displayed mostly in war, which was not likely to stop in the city states of his time, and his considered corrective was the large middle class, because he was aware in his *Politics* that you cannot rely on every kind of state having the right virtues. The Stoics were the ones who mentioned an army as not being necessary in an ideal society. But an ideal society and the disbanding of armies would be the joint products of an imaginary community of the wise, which had not been realized. The Stoics would not think it could be realized by Aristotle's recipe of moderation.

In the recent discourse, I think, the term 'moderates' in the context of warfare has proven to be rather unhelpful, because it conceals the actual motivations of parties caught up in a conflict and labels them only in terms of whether you think them more likely to side with you to some extent.

RJ: But you would not be suspicious of the term 'moderation' when this concept is used by non-violent thinkers like Gandhi and Martin Luther King Jr?

RS: No. Did Gandhi and Martin Luther King Jr give prominence to that word?

RJ: They both use it from time to time. They think moderating one's temper means that your emotions do not get over you, especially when you have the ability to use violence.

RS: I don't know whether Gandhi would have preferred Aristotle's moderation of anger to the Stoic eradication. He was very severe with himself about his tendency to anger.

Part VI

Animals and Humans

Animal Minds and Human Morals

RJ: One of your books, which I read with a lot of interest, is on the subject of animal ethics. What brought you to write about animal ethics?

RS: I call the book *Animal Minds and Human Morals* (1995), and at first, I was interested only in animal minds. That was because I had been studying the Stoic view on that, and I had been surprised that they spent so much time trying to prove that animals were none of them rational. Now, it seems to me from animal studies untrue that none are rational, and I thought how funny it is that these rather good Stoic philosophers spent so much energy trying to prove their claim. Then I realized that there was an ethical reason: They were defending the standard Greek practice of sacrificing animals to the Gods and also eating them. In fact, typically, if you bought meat from the butcher, it was likely that it would come from a sacrifice, and they were defending that practice by insisting on this theory of animal minds. By contrast, their view of humans was that we owe justice to them all, because all are rational. That included foreigners, people who can't speak Greek, the barbarians who just say 'bar-bar', slaves, even though they were usually considered mere property that you could damage if you chose. We owe justice to all. To say that all are rational is not to say that all think right. But they all have concepts, and having concepts, they can reason, badly perhaps in many cases, but no animals can. So we owe nothing to animals; we can continue sacrificing and killing them, and using them for our own purposes. I realized it was no good writing a book about animal minds; I had to write a book about animal minds and human morals. One of the Neoplatonists, Porphyry, in the third century CE wrote a beautiful book, *On Abstinence from Killing Animals*, in reply to the Stoics, in support of animals and against killing them. He was the first Neoplatonic commentator on Aristotle and he divided his book into four parts, called books, though we would call them chapters. In Book One, he surveys the entire Greek controversy about whether or not it is all right to kill animals. It was much more evenly matched than in the Christian tradition, because Christ ate meat, and his disciples were fishermen. The controversy includes remarkable reconstructions of the development of civilization and the origins of sacrificing and killing animals. In Book Two, Porphyry looks at the nature of God or the gods. They are immaterial beings, and so do not want physical bodies sacrificed to them. God wants the sacrifice of a pure mind. It sounds almost like Christianity. Material sacrifice of animals simply attracts to you the evil demons, who take on bodily shapes and are the ones who love it. Book Three turns from gods to animals themselves. Do they satisfy the criterion of his Stoic opponents for being owed justice—that is, are animals rational? I have been convinced by the recent work of Fay Edwards that rationality is not Porphyry's own criterion for who is owed justice. If we take the Stoic criterion for deserving justice, there are lots of animals who meet their requirement of rationality. Porphyry reared a partridge when he was in Carthage, and the partridge learnt special Porphyry-speak instead of partridge-speak, surely a sign of rationality, he said. Book Four is about other cultures including the Brahmins in India. There were many other cultures too, the Essene Jews and others, who are vegetarian and don't eat animals, and they don't suffer in any way at all. He surveys these cultures. So it's a very beautiful, impressive, and well-argued book in favour of animals. Animal sacrifice, and the consequent eating, was very much a part of the religious life in Greek cities, and so Porphyry requires abstinence only from philosophers. Fay Edwards has convinced me that this is because from the time of Plato's *Phaedo* onwards, Platonist philosophers are expected to try to purify themselves, like Socrates, from bodily desires.

Animals and Moral Philosophy

RJ: Aristotle denies that animals have belief and reasoning, but he admits that animals have perception. As for the Stoics, they allow animals to have perceptual appearances with propositional content, but suggest that the main difference between humans and animals is that animals lack reason. Did they base this on animals lacking syntax?

RS: I think the argument I caricatured as 'They lack syntax, so we can eat them' was a modern argument. As the attempts at a blanket distinction of all animals from humans failed, we reached that point. But it is said that the grey parrot has syntax. It was something slightly different that the Stoics said. They said that animals don't have reason, but they defined reason in an unusual way, as having concepts. Aristotle had allowed very rudimentary concepts to animals. He uses a special name for it: 'experience'. It was equivalent to having many memories; if you had many memories of oxen, then you had a rudimentary concept of oxen, but it is not a scientific concept. But the Stoics didn't allow animals any concepts and so didn't allow them reason.

RJ: Did you talk about the absence of moral reasoning?

RS: It wasn't only moral reasoning. The Stoic idea was that animals didn't have any form of reasoning.

RJ: In your book you try to answer some of the new discussions of animal rights. You make a very persuasive case that the present worry about animal rights needs a different philosophical backing. What do you think are the philosophical weaknesses of these points of view in relation to animals?

RS: Well, I do admire the people who speak up for animals, even while I'm not convinced by the grounds they gave at the time I wrote. I think Peter Singer, who gave what I call a utilitarian argument, has had a marvellous effect on the better treatment of animals; I think his work has increased the number of vegetarians among younger people. It is very noticeable in universities that the student generation has started in much larger numbers to be vegetarian, as the kitchens will tell you. I think Peter Singer's work brought a lot of this about, so I congratulate him. It is not only his argument, but also the other main argument against harming animals at the time I wrote that looked for just one thing that matters in each case. Singer's one consideration was *preference satisfaction*. He rightly said that animals have preferences, just as we do. One obvious preference is not being killed, but animals have lots of preferences. It can then be argued that there would be more total satisfaction of preferences if you took into account animal preferences as well as human preferences, and that makes it wrong to harm animals. What worries me is not the conclusion, but that I don't think it is true that there's only one thing that matters. We have discussed this in the very different context of Gandhi. In his case I was saying that, just as with Christ, it's probably very necessary that they think there are only very few things that matter, because they have got to refocus attention, and not to mind a lot of things, in order to achieve the great things they achieved. Well, animals provide another context in which people are saying there's really one criterion that matters, of right and wrong, and I don't think it's true. The second main argument at the time I wrote that appealed to a single criterion of right and wrong was that animals have rights. They have rights because they have certain valuable characteristics. What are these characteristics? Well, they have certain forms of consciousness, rather difficult to define because animals are different from each other, and you have got to find one that is morally relevant. You don't want something like 'Some of them understand syntax', because that's irrelevant to whether to kill them. What I wrote was that I don't think there is only one thing that matters. I think there are so many reasons that you should think about in how to treat animals. What is being left out? Take first one small question: There may be handicapped human children who have less reason than animals. We still don't kill them, because we are related to them in the most intimate way, and it's a tragedy that they don't have the capacities of their parents and the rest of us. It's a tragedy, and that is a further consideration. Again, you have run over the leg of an animal while driving your car; have you killed it? Oh, it's only an animal, so you don't stop. But wait a moment, another consideration here is that it was you who ran it over, so you have incurred a certain responsibility. The man in the next car doesn't have the same responsibility. If he is a very decent person, he too might stop and see how the animal is doing. But you have a particular responsibility, because it was you who ran the animal over. There are hundreds and hundreds of reasons to bring to bear, not just one. Whether an animal feels *pain* may be more important than whether it has certain higher forms of consciousness that we admire. If you ran over a log which didn't suffer in any way, it wouldn't matter in the same way. That is my approach to ethics. There are hundreds of considerations. It is a very good thing to sort them out and think which are the most important, be ready to forever consider new ones, forever expanding your imagination: Here are considerations I have never thought of before. I must add those to my repertoire, and look out for new considerations. The more considerations you're aware of, the better. So I am against the one-criterion approach to ethics. But I say that in a spirit of admiration for philosophers who have stood up for animals. Peter Singer had additional influence because he gave a lot of empirical evidence of how badly we treat animals. I guess that weighed as much as the philosophical argument, and we owe a great deal to him.

My search for multiple considerations led me to make some concessions to the other side of the debate. I thought that you would owe special loyalty to your own kind, if there were an insoluble clash between its welfare and that of other kinds. Suppose there were powerful Martians who could survive only by eating us. I would not characterize their doing so as *unjust*, although I would think it was to be avoided, and by killing them if possible. Again, I distinguished between serious grounds of medical research for humans to kill animals, if there were no alternative, and merely cosmetic grounds. This was no doubt just as well for me, since later for medical reasons I found I was not getting enough protein, and so I gave up my temporary compromise on eating habits, although the temporary experience had led me to prefer a far less meaty diet than I had been brought up with and to enjoy a flexible diet.

Gandhi and Animals

RJ: Since you have mentioned Gandhi, maybe we should go back to the readings of Eastern traditions in relation to the treatment of animals. I think the Western world needs to read a little bit more on how the Eastern civilizations have portrayed animal ethics.

RS: Well, Gandhi was very thoughtful and we can learn from him. In the ashram communities which he ran, little children were running around, but there were snakes. There were also monkeys stealing the crops on which they depended, often for fun, not to eat them. What do you do with the monkeys? He brought everyone together to discuss whether to kill them or, as was decided, to remove them. There was the case of the 60 stray dogs, which might be rabid. Gandhi produced outrage among his followers of non-violence when he endorsed the decision of the municipal council to shoot them. Because the municipal councillors had undertaken responsibility for the safety of the citizens, their duty to kill the dogs overrode the fact that the violence against the dogs remained wrong. Reneging on their undertaking would be even worse, he said. Gandhi was taking into account multiple considerations, in this case the undertaking to the city's population. At the same time, the openness of his discussion was remarkable. He published in 1926 outspoken objections to himself (he even called one violent) from the followers of non-violence in his internationally read newspapers and he formulated an illuminating revision, over the course of seven articles, of his definition of non-violence, although in no way denying that the treatment of the dogs was violent.

The Masters and Possessors of Nature

RJ: When we compare Eastern philosophies with Western philosophies, I think that the anti-animal perspective prevails in the West, starting from the Greeks.

RS: Yes, I have mentioned that that was true to a large extent of the Christian tradition, partly because of the diet of Christ and his disciples. But it was very different with the ancient Greeks, among whom the debate was evenly matched.

RJ: Not the Greeks, but definitely with St Augustine up to modern times. Don't you think it is directly related to a line of thought which is that of the domination of Nature by human beings that we find in Descartes, when he talks about the human being as the master and possessor of Nature?

RS: You are right that this is an element. In the story of Creation in the Hebrew book of Genesis, inherited by the Christians, when God gave humans dominion over animals, that did not at first include eating them, since he gave them as food only vegetation (1:28–9). But animals as food were explicitly added by God in a covenant with Noah, who had saved animals from the great flood, though not before Noah had offered God burnt offerings of animals (8:20–9:3), and before him Abel had sacrificed animals to God (4:3–5). So the Judaeo–Christian tradition certainly endorses the idea you cite of dominion over animals allowing before long the killing of them. Among the Greeks, the idea that animals exist for humans is ascribed to Socrates, is explicit in Aristotle, who justifies hunting them, and is taken to the furthest extreme by the Stoic Chrysippus, although a more central argument for the Stoics is the supposed non-rationality of all animals. The Jewish thinker Philo of Alexandria, writing in Greek, endorses the dominion view, which he knows from both sources. Nonetheless, there were replies to the dominion argument even within the Judaeo–Christian tradition by the Christians Basil of Caesarea and John Chrysostom in the fourth century CE, and by the Jewish philosopher Maimonides in the twelfth century CE. There continued to be individual defenders of animals among the Christian saints, among whom the best known is Saint Francis either side of 1200 CE, who was followed by the ensuing Franciscan tradition, although even he has been accused of not objecting to the cutting off of a pig's trotters.

In the ancient Greek tradition, there were strong defenders of animals before Porphyry, on several of whom he draws. Defenders of animals had included the Greek Pythagorean tradition, Porphyry's own Platonist tradition, and most surprisingly, Aristotle's successor, Theophrastus, who appears to disagree with Aristotle. An early argument was based on reincarnation, in which the Pythagoreans and Plato believed. Pythagoras, teaching before 500 BCE, is said to have forbidden the beating of a dog, because he could recognize a friend's voice in it. Empedocles was very close to Pythagoreans, he too not much after 500 BCE. He claimed to remember having been incarnated as a boy, girl, bird, fish, and even as a bush. He regarded himself as suffering reincarnations for 30,000 years as a punishment for having eaten animals, because they are our reincarnated kin. Hence, in sacrificing and eating them, father is slaying son, children their mother. I must ask you if this theme is pursued in Hinduism.

Animals in the Indian Tradition

RJ: In Indian religious traditions, animals are sacred and they can be represented as half-gods, like Ganesha. But we don't have the same conceptions in Judaism, Islam, or Christianity.

RS: That is true, although sacredness is not a guarantee of care. But when I first went to India, animals gave me one of my first lessons in the need to rethink unchallenged assumptions. I was initially surprised by seeing dead cows on the road, because you don't see many dead animals on the road in England. But then I realized why you don't. It is because people take their sick pet animals to the veterinary surgeon and have them humanely killed, though they would refuse to do that to their relatives. I needed to ask myself, then: Is the English treatment of pet animals more humane, or how far is it for convenience? I am not advocating the latter conclusion, merely illustrating the need to avoid complacency.

The Stoics and Animals

RJ: Let us stay on this. I am sure that you have also come up with this contradiction among the Stoics, who have the concept of universal community and who treat masters and slaves as equally our kin, but have this denigration of animals. Do you see a contradiction there?

RS: It's not a contradiction, but their reason for making such a sharp difference between the treatment of humans and of animals is doubly mistaken. First of all, whether animals have reason is not really relevant to how you should treat them. Whether they feel pain is much more relevant, and of course, there are multiple other considerations: farm animals may have served you all their lives, for example. The second flaw is that it is false, in my view, that no animals have reason.

RJ: There is one subject that is very important and you have not written about, and that is in relation to cannibalism. There have been cases of cannibalism in human civilization, not only as a cultural or ritual practice, but also as a means of survival—like the football team that had to survive for 72 days in the Andes after a plane crash and had to eat the dead bodies of their comrades. It is a moral choice that is related very closely to the survival of the body.

RS: Assuming that the other people were dead, I have no problems with it in those particular extreme circumstances.

Is Cannibalism a Moral Attitude?

RJ: But how about cannibalism as a whole?

RS: It would be quite different to eat the limbs of the dead except in extremities. It would show a disrespect for the memory of fellow humans instead of the fellow-feeling which the Stoics particularly advocated. The Greeks discussed several scenarios. The suggestion that one might eat the limbs of one's own dead parents would be correspondingly worse. Killing the living to eat them would be worse again. None of these objections applied to the case of the survivors in extremities eating the dead.

RJ: What were the moral and philosophical views of ancient Greeks with regard to cannibalism?

RS: Theophrastus, Aristotle's successor, is reported in Porphyry's book *On Abstinence from Killing Animals* as saying that cannibalism first arose to replace vegetarianism as a result of famine, and that the eating of animals was a replacement of cannibalism. Theophrastus uses the suggested origin of eating animals to discredit it as equally unnatural. The early Cynic school and the early Stoic school which developed out of it may not have agreed on what was unnatural. At any rate, Diogenes the Cynic and Chrysippus, the third Stoic head, are alleged by possibly hostile sources to have said that eating the limbs even of your deceased parents, and, in extreme circumstances, eating others alive is permissible. This appears to contrast with the Stoic insistence on human fellow-feeling, but if they said it, it will have been one of the several examples of these schools rejecting convention in favour of what is alleged to be natural, and that will have been the rationale. There is no afterlife, and the dead body has become a matter of indifference. On the case of eating the living in extreme circumstances, however, the description of Chrysippus suggests he was embarrassed, saying that the wise Stoic will *even* eat human flesh in certain circumstances.

Philosophers and the Support for Animals

RJ: In your book, there is a voluntary neglect of the Bible and of the chapter on Genesis. In Genesis, there is a human dominance over natural species. You also ignore the medieval and modern philosophers who are on the side of the animals, like Schopenhauer.

RS: I think I did mention all of these in my book, but no doubt too briefly. I recorded the treatment in Genesis of meat-eating. I mentioned a number of medieval Christian thinkers who supported animals, and those that I just mentioned were some of them. I did also mention Schopenhauer, and said that he praised the English, who, in 1839 when he wrote, had recently founded a Society for the Prevention of Cruelty to Animals. He saw the English as a happy exception to the general denial of rights to animals on the mistaken ground of irrationality.

Part VII

Looking Back

Reminiscing

RJ: We are practically at the end of this book, and I would like to ask you a few personal questions. When you look back at the 80 years of your life, especially to half a century of scholarly life and research, up to what point do you see yourself as a modern Stoic or as someone who has been influenced by the Stoics, passionate about them, and who has been influenced directly by their state of mind?

RS: Well, I have not yet been put to one of the great Stoic tests, the loss of health, and so it may be premature to speak. But I can say already that I don't live up to the Stoic ideals of invulnerability, and to the extent that it involves detachment, I would not wish to try. But I certainly have been influenced. In our earlier talk on reading the Greeks, we discussed being a Stoic today, and I picked out six Stoic ideas that impressed me. Certain aspects of them suited my temperament, but in other respects, such as that of detachment from all emotional reaction, I should not want to be like them. It's rather that I think there are certain emotions that are damaging or distressing and too often exercised when it is not necessary. To some extent, admittedly, they cannot be separated from the good emotions, and then they are necessary. How can you have a lovely relationship without distress at bereavement? It is inadvisable to try. I'm not with them there. But for avoiding emotion at little ups and downs that otherwise spoil the day, they are very good guides.

RJ: But if you were born in a Hindu or a Muslim family in India, would you still think that at some point in your life you would be attracted to Stoicism or you would have been more attracted to Islam and Hinduism?

RS: Well, I hope I would do what Gandhi recommended, and what, in a very small way, I have tried to do. My Indian family devoted their whole lives to behaving with sympathy for faiths other than their own. Having grown up in such a family, I've taken a great interest in faiths with which I was not particularly familiar, and I hope that if I were a Hindu or a Muslim, I would have done that the other way around. I think it's a useful thing to do, because I agree with Gandhi that no religion has all the truth. I also agree with Gandhi that it is normally completely unnecessary to totally abandon the religion in which you have grown up. There may be some bad practices which you should give up, but the Dalai Lama, just like Gandhi, also tells people not to convert. What Gandhi did was to borrow from other faiths, to question some ideas in his own, to reinterpret all faiths, but not suddenly to sweep everything away or suddenly convert to something else that he still had to learn. I am a borrower in philosophy and I am a borrower in religion.

An Intercultural Philosopher

RJ: Yes, you are a borrower but you are also an intercultural mind, who, I would permit myself to say, is not very British.

The British philosophers have a lot of assets but they are certainly not intercultural. They are very deeply rooted in their own philosophical and intellectual culture. This is not your case.

RS: Well, I'm glad to hear you say that, because I don't want it to be my case. I think there are difficulties about university curricula which tend to make one concentrate on a particular canon of writers, easiest if the origin is of your own language of course. I think there are certain inevitable distortions here and we should do our best to try and counteract them. Sir Isaiah Berlin, however, lifted people's gaze beyond the curriculum of his time in Oxford, as I have said, and some universities do very well in broadening the curriculum. But I think we need more people like you, if I may return the compliment, to make us think about other cultures.

Being Reborn and Choices in Life

RJ: My last question. You certainly don't believe in reincarnation, but if you were reborn, would you again like to be a philosopher who had studied at Oxford and worked on ancient philosophers?

RS: There is nothing I would like particularly different about my life because I feel lucky. But to stick just to my work, which is only one part of my life, there are only some things I would like to keep constant. Because I find the world intellectually fascinating, I would like, if possible, still to have intellectual interests, and in that case, I think it would be a pity not to learn new things. There is so much to learn and understand. Of course, I would regret the thought, if there was going to be no influence from what I had learnt in the present incarnation, but the Indian theory allows the reborn to build on that influence. Which new thing to learn would depend on the abilities with which one was reborn. If I were reborn good enough at mathematics, I would be glad to study the cosmology of the universe.

I would also hope to be reborn in a period or place where one is free to form one's own views. I have lived in such environments, and I referred earlier to other periods in which inquiry was free and intercultural. One was the period in which Greek philosophy was transferred partly via Christians in Syria, to Arabic-speaking centuries in which Muslims and Christians alike were free to take the subject very much further and to debate views which might or might not fit with theological orthodoxy. The milieu should be different but I would like it to be an exciting one, such as I have had the pleasure to enjoy here, and I know there have been others.

RJ: Would you have liked to spend more time in India?

RS: In one way, I would. There's a limit to how much you can attend to and I think it is quite important to know something extremely well. I knew Greek and Latin first reasonably well, and then Greek and Roman philosophies. That was an accident of the time I was brought up where Greek and Latin was the most prestigious subject. It was a perfectly happy accident. My knowledge of India was inevitably small by comparison, even though I longed to know more about India. I started with a quite illusory picture, since I knew about princely India, just the extremely exotic. My aunts told me a great deal about it and I regaled my schoolmates with the stories. But it was only in retirement that I was able to really find out much. Before that, it was only in middle age that I had the money to take my family to India. So I think it was inevitable that I couldn't become comparably knowledgeable about it. There are people like Darwin, geniuses who can become brilliant in many spheres, but I'm not one of those. I can only become reasonably knowledgeable about one thing. So if I benefitted from reincarnation, I would be very happy for it to be in India, but I would hope that from India I would again have the reverse ability to learn about another culture. So I don't regret it wasn't

India first. I rejoice that I have little time left to learn more about India, although India is so vast that I have to accept that it will only be a little bit. Ancient Greek has the great advantages of being in the past, and there are only so many million words of ancient Greek surviving. So with ancient Greek and Latin philosophy, you can learn about some reasonable proportion. You can't do that with modern English literature, for example, because we have got so much writing left. Much less could you do it with all the languages of India.

RJ: Professor Sorabji, thank you for your time.

RS: Thank you for making me think about new questions on old thoughts. It's been a very good experience.

About the Author

Born in Tehran, Iran, in 1956, Ramin Jahanbegloo, an Iranian–Canadian philosopher, has worked extensively to foster constructive dialogue between divergent cultures. In his efforts to promote argumentative tradition, he has interacted with scholars and intellectuals from all over the world: the Dalai Lama, Noam Chomsky, Ashis Nandy, and George Steiner among others. In recent years, he invited Richard Rorty, Timothy Garton Ash, Antonio Negri, and Michael Ignatieff, and many intellectuals to Iran.

In late April 2006, on his way to an international conference in Brussels, Ramin was arrested by the Iranian authorities. On 19 May, more than 400 prominent intellectuals, including Nobel laureates, scholars, and human rights activists, in an open letter demanded his immediate release. Among the undersigned were: Noam Chomsky, J.M. Coetzee, Shirin Ebadi, Umberto Eco, Jürgen Habermas, Timothy Garton Ash, Leszek Kołakowski, Antonio Negri, Richard Rorty, Krzysztof Zanussi, and Howard Zinn. On 30 August he was released from prison after four months of confinement.

In 2006 and 2007 Ramin was Rajni Kothari Professor of Democracy at the Centre for the Study of Developing Societies (CSDS) in New Delhi, India. He won the peace prize from the United Nations Association in Spain for his extensive academic works in promoting dialogue between cultures and his advocacy for non-violence. He is also on the advisory board of PEN Canada.

A film buff, Ramin is a bibliophile. He is presently an Associate Professor and York-Noor Chair in Islamic Studies at York University. *Talking Philosophy* is his seventh book with OUP.